Book and CD

The Complete
Voice & Speech Workout

The Documentation and Recording of an Oral
Tradition for the Purpose of Training and Practices

Edited by
Janet B. Rodgers

Exercises contributed by
members of the Voice and Speech
Trainers Association

APPLAUSE
THEATRE & CINEMA BOOKS
An Imprint of Hal Leonard Corporation

Edited by Janet Rodgers
Copyright © 2002 by Janet Rodgers

Published in 2002 by Applause Theatre & Cinema Books
An Imprint of Hal Leonard Corporation
7777 West Bluemound Road
Milwaukee, WI 53213

Trade Book Division Editorial Offices
33 Plymouth Street, Montclair, NJ 07042

Library of Congress Cataloging-in-Publication Data
        Library of Congress Control Number: 2002102525

British Library Cataloging-in-Publication Data
        A catalog record for this book is available from the British Library

ISBN: 978-1-55783-498-0

www.applausepub.com

Table of Contents

*Location of exercise on accompanying CD

**Location of
exercise on
accompanying CD*

**Location of
exercise on
accompanying CD*

Acknowledgements

Thank you to the fifty-four members of the Voice and Speech Trainers Association who contributed exercises for this book. Special thanks to Ann Furniss, Kim McQuillan, and Elizabeth Brinkley, for their word processing help; Mandy Rees and Jeffrey Smart, for their input on structure; Phil Timberlake, for his research and for lending his voice for the CD; and John Heroy and the Virginia Commonwealth University School of the Arts, for awarding me a Faculty Research Leave Grant. I'd like to thank my department chair, David Leong and my colleagues in the Theatre Department at Virginia Commonwealth University for their continued support over the years. And last, but not least, I'd like to thank my husband, Christus Murphy, and my son, Jonathan, for their never-ending patience, support, and love, my father, Lionel, for his inspiration, and my dear mother, Margaret Hyde Rodgers, for lending her discerning eye and ear.

Introduction

How To Use This Book

The impetus for putting this book together came from an exercise I had always known as, "The Joshua Steele Exercise." I had been doing this exercise with my students for about thirty years when I discovered that the exercise had been in existence since the 18th century. It intrigued me to think of actors performing an exercise which had existed for over 200 years. The discovery occurred during the same time that the Voice and Speech Trainers Association was having an exercise swap session at its yearly conference. I began to wonder how many other exercises we were doing that had been handed down over the years from actor to actor and from teacher to teacher via an oral tradition. So I decided to set about collecting exercises in an attempt to document a tradition which has up to this point been communicated primarily by word of mouth.

This book contains 74 voice and speech exercises which have been submitted by members of the Voice and Speech Trainers Association (VASTA).* I have grouped the exercises in each chapter according to each exercise's primary purpose. I have then arranged the chapters following the progression you might use if you were an actor warming up your voice before a performance or for a performance class. The exercises from Chapter One, "Getting to Know Your Voice," are intended for classroom use only. If you are an actor working alone, you will want to explore the exercises from Chapters 2-7. You will find many of these exercises recorded on the CD which accompanies this book. These exercises take the body and voice on a journey; from being in a quiet and centered place through contacting the breath, making sound, exploring pitch and projection, and, finally, calling with a full, extended voice. By selecting exercises from Chapters 2-7, you can create a wonderful, healthy, sequential vocal warm-up for either yourself or for a class. The exercises in Chapter 8 integrate voice and text while the exercises in Chapter 9 integrate voice and body. The final chapter of the book explores acoustical adjustments of the voice, both character voices and dialects.

All of the exercises have been written in the "teacher's voice" as if s/he were "teaching the material for the first time." This book is intended to be used by professional voice users (actors, singers, and public speakers) as well as teachers of theatre and directors. Some of the exercises are appropriate for an individual working alone (solo exercises) and some are more conducive to classroom use (group exercises). Many of the solo exercises can be adapted to group or classroom work.

---

*The Voice and Speech Trainers Association, VASTA, was born in August, 1986. Its several hundred international members from around the world are teachers, scientists, vocal coaches, actors, directors, and recognized specialists in private practice. Other VASTA monographs published by Applause Books are *Standard Speech and Other Contemporary Issues in Professional Voice and Speech Training*, *The Voice in Violence* (both edited by Rocco DalVera), and *A Vocal Vision* (edited by Marian Hampton and Barbara Acker).

Chapter I

Getting to Know Your Voice

The exercises in this chapter are designed to be used in a voice and speech class during the first few weeks of the course. From Betsy Argo's exercise, "Sign-In" (1-1) and Kristen Loree's "The Name Game" (1-3), which help break down physical and vocal inhibitions as students introduce themselves to new classmates, to Robert Barton's, "The Voice Speaks" (1-2), which encourages students to personify their voices, to Lynn Watson's "Tell Me About the Time You…"(1-4), which helps connect breath with imagery, all of these exercises are group exercises which foster self expression.

During the first few classroom sessions, it is important to establish an atmosphere of openness and freedom in which positive, constructive criticism can take place. The four exercises in this chapter allow for self-expression and creativity while giving students and teachers opportunities to get to know one another. Voice and speech training touches the core of our being and a positive environment is of utmost importance in order for growth and change to take place.

All of the exercises in the following chapter attempt to lay the foundation for the vocal skills which the actor or professional voice user must have in order to give full vocal expression to the text. When we listen to our voice on a recording, we are frequently disappointed or embarrassed: "That doesn't sound like me!" Well, in reality, your recorded voice probably sounds more like you than you think it does. Take time to let your emotions settle and then listen again with an objective ear. Try to understand what it is that you don't like about your voice. Does your voice sound strangled or constricted (perhaps too much muscular tension)? Is your voice thin (lacking in resonance)? Is the pitch monotone (all on one note and lacking pitch variety)? Does your voice lack power (lack of breath support)? Do your words sound mumbled (weak articulation)? Are the vowels flat (tone placement not in the front of the mouth)? The exercises in the chapter that follows are designed to provide a workout for your voice. If you can analyze the problem, then you can find a solution. It is always best to find a voice and speech trainer who can help you set up a workout which best suits your needs. Then, just as with a full body physical workout, it all comes down to following a daily routine.

Sign-in

Purposes of the Exercise

To stretch the body

To connect with breath

To expand volume

To extend pitch range

To project or extend sound

To clarify speech

A Brief History of the Exercise:

This exercise is perhaps a combination of work I've done with Viola Spolin exercises and Arthur Lessac. I created this exercise to break down physical inhibitions in voice and body movements as students introduce themselves to new classmates. This exercise also gives me an opportunity to assess vocal and/or bodily hang-ups, strengths and/or weaknesses in public presentation. — **Betsy Argo**

THE EXERCISE

1. Hello. Since most of us are meeting each other for the first time, I would like each of you to stand up and spell out your first names, letter by letter in the air, using your right or left hand, depending on whether you are a "lefty" or a "righty." Using your entire body, make the letters as big as you can by comfortably bending and stretching as far as possible.

2. Since cursive writing works best for joining the letters, you will try to use only one breath to sustain all the letters in your name. Then, when you have completed signing all the letters in the air, take a large breath. Give a big cheerleader-like jump into the air, raise your arms above your head, and clearly pronounce your name in a hearty shout at the same time.

3. I will demonstrate. *(At which point I spell out B-E-T-S-Y, yell my name, and end with a reasonably high jump into the air.)* Okay, let's go right down the line.

4. Are we all "signed in?" Good! How did that feel? Were you out of breath before you finished the longer names, etc.? Who do you think demonstrated the greatest variety in voice, in body movement, etc.? Who jumped the highest?

The Voice Speaks

Purpose of the Exercise

To help students personify their voices in order to develop a relationship/friendship with their own voices

A Brief History of the Exercise:

Some of my students didn't seem to like their own voices and many regarded their voices as unreliable, perhaps even adversarial. So I designed a series of exercises (including whimsical activities such as drawing and coloring one's voice) of which this is a part. It reminds me of an old TV animated commercial for an antacid product where a person and his stomach (represented by separate drawings) are trying to reach an agreement, and when they do, the stomach climbs happily back inside the person. — **Robert Barton**

THE EXERCISE

1. Let your voice reveal its name to you and what it would look like, how it would present itself in a visual form, how it would move, and what its attitude would be if it had the chance to speak separately from you. Sleep on this. Let the answers come to you. Put yourself in a place of deep empathy for your voice. What is it like to be inside you and serving you? Do you ever abuse your voice with screaming, smoking, lack of hydration, etc.? What is life like being your voice?

2. Consider what clothing to wear and how to wear it the day of the presentation. The clothing should visually personify your voice.

3. Consider where and how you would locate yourself in the room. Do you want to crawl under a platform, climb through the window, roll through the door? Do you want to hide under a hood or hat and then reveal yourself? Do you want to storm into the room and shout because you are so glad to have the chance? Or sneak in and then gradually assert yourself? Let all of the possibilities emerge from your own imagination and history with your voice.

4. On the day of presentation, when it is your turn, leave the room as yourself and return as your voice. Complete the following statements:

   My name is _____. I live inside _____
   _____. The two best words or phrases to describe
   me would be: _ _____ and _____ .
   I am the biggest help to _____
   by _____.
   I give him/her a bad time by _____.
   Sometimes I wish _____ would just ____
   _____
   _____ .

The Name Game

Purposes of the Exercise

To release the brain muscles

To learn the names of class members

To get the body moving with the voice

A Brief History of the Exercise:

At NYU (where I got my MFA in acting) the voice teacher, Beverly Wideman, played a sound poem game which I then turned into the name game. I find that getting the muscle memory working while looking at each person, saying their name, and following their movements is quite useful for retention of information. — **Kristen Loree**

THE EXERCISE

1. Remove your shoes and come stand in a circle.

2. We are going to play a name game to get to know each other better, and also to loosen up our bodies a bit.

3. I'm going to start. I'm going to say my name and link it to a movement. There will be one movement per syllable.

4. Once I've created mine, you will rehearse it three times. Watch and listen closely. Make sure to do exactly what I've done, not what you wanted me to do or what you think I should have done.

5. Next, we will move to the person on my left, who will start their movement from wherever I left off. So if I am on all fours, they start there. That way you cannot plan what you're going to do. Your movement will be a spontaneous response to where we are.

6. We will rehearse three times and then go back to the beginning. Then add the next person's movement, rehearse, and start again from the top.

7. It will be fun. You will sweat. Keep your eyes on the person who's created the movement — he or she is your cue. Make sure as you rehearse, that all the details (lefts and rights, hand position, pitch, etc.) are attended to. Now, let's all find neutral and inhale together.

Note: *This can also become a theme game, a storytelling game, an emotion game, or any other kind of sound/movement exploration you'd like. Play! Have fun.*

Tell Me About the Time You...

Purposes of the Exercise

To connect with breath

To connect breath with
imagery and text

A Brief History of the Exercise:

I learned the original version of this from Bob Hobbs as an acting exercise. It has been modified for use as a vocal exercise. — **Lynn Watson**

THE EXERCISE

Pre-Exercise Preparation:

Ask one student to sit in a chair, facing the class. This student is called Mr./Ms. X.

1. To Mr./Ms. X: I am going to ask you to tell the class about an extraordinary event you experienced. Then, I want you to improvise your version of what happened, reliving it moment by moment. The improvisation must build in energy and intensity as it progresses. You will be seated as you begin to talk about the event, but feel free to let the energy of your involvement pull you out of the chair, using more space as you become fully, physically engaged in your portrayal.

2. While Mr./Ms. X is telling us about the event, I want those of you in the rest of the class to take notes on what you observe about the actor's voice and physicality.

3. Now, get ready. "Mr./Ms. X, tell me about the time you were swept out to sea   ."

   The instructor suggests the subject matter for the event, so that the exercise stimulates the way an actor must inhabit and commit to the imaginary life of a scripted character.

   The actor is not to worry if their descriptions become outrageous or illogical. The rules of improvisation apply – say "yes" to whatever comes up, don't block, fully commit to the most outrageous choices/ideas, etc.

Note: *The improvisation should run about 3-5 minutes — longer if the student needs to be coached in intensity and physical commitment. The instructor can side-coach by asking questions about the event and, if necessary, help bring the improvisation to a close.*

Tell Me About the Time You...

FOLLOW-UP

Post-Exercise Discussion:
(Occurs after each student performs.)

1. Let's talk about what you observed during the exercise. When you were performing, what did you notice about your voice, speech, and physicality? When you were in the audience, what did you notice about the voice, speech, and physicality of the actors?

2. What did you notice about the range of vocal dynamics that were used? What did you notice about pitch, tempo, volume, and voice qualities?

3. What about the way images were relied upon to provide given circumstances? Were they believable? Energetic? Spontaneous?

4. Can you remember how strong the eye focus was as the actor relied on images to help him/her develop his/her situations and to naturally trigger strong vocal/physical responses?

5. Why do you think the images the actor was "seeing" seemed so real? Do you think it could be because they were very specifically located in the space around the actor – high, low, in front, to the side, near, far, etc.? Often, the actor's image was so strong that we felt that we could "see" what the actor was "seeing." How often is that true when we go to a play?

6. When the actor was connecting to images did you notice that it triggered a strong, connected use of breath, which was in turn spontaneously connected (without holding or pre-planning) to the release of text? What kind of unexpected and interesting physicalities were triggered by the strong connection to image and breath?

7. So, after doing this exercise, do you think images are effective in triggering emotional responses that flow outward through the breath, voice, and body?

8. Now, let's discuss ways in which discoveries from this exercise might be implemented by you to improve your acting.

Chapter 2

Stretching, Centering, Releasing, and Aligning

Life in the 21st century places stresses upon the muscles of the body that can result in an excess of muscular tension. The body needs to be working at its optimum in order for full vocal expression to occur. Driving an automobile means that our arms are held in a outward position and our head frequently juts forward for long periods of time. Getting stuck in traffic can increase the muscular tension in our face, jaw, shoulders, neck and arms. Likewise, sitting at a computer, if we are not careful about how we sit, can lead to muscular stress which can have a profound effect on the tension level in our body. Unless we make a concerted effort to counterbalance this stress, our bodies may get "unbalanced" and we may feel "uncentered," "out of balance," or "stressed out."

The exercises in this chapter are designed to help bring the stressed-out muscles into a state of release and our bodies into alignment. When our muscles are at optimum balance between stress and release, our bones are in alignment, and the vocal sounds we make are able to resonate fully in our body. When the head, neck, ribcage, pelvis, and legs are in optimal alignment, the channel for breath and sound is open, free, and unencumbered.

"Neck Stretches" (2-1) addresses the muscles in the neck and shoulders. "Rest Position" (2-2) focuses on releasing the tongue. "Side Stretches at the Barre" (2-3) is based on ballet form and combines stretching the ribcage while breathing with gliding sound. "Advanced Triangle Pose" (2-4) presents a modified yoga exercise which stretches the intercostal muscles as breath moves fully into the ribcage. "Balance and Alignment Using the Wall" (2-5) concentrates on the spine. Massage as a method for releasing muscular tension is the focus of "12 Step Program for Release of Neck, Jaws, and Shoulders" (2-6). For "Tennis Ball Torture" (2-7), you will need two tennis balls and a soft mat.

Neck Stretches

Purpose of the Exercise

To stretch and release the neck and shoulder muscles

A Brief History of the Exercise:

I learned this from my chiropractor, Eric Carlson, D.C. — **Lynx Brammer**

THE EXERCISE

This neck stretch is performed from a supported erect position.

You may sit or stand, but make sure that your body is in good posture with the spine in alignment.

1. Keeping your chin parallel to the ground, slowly turn your head as far to the right as you can. Hold this stretch. (This and all steps of the stretch are held for three to five seconds.)

2. Slowly allow your head to float back to center keeping your chin parallel to the ground.

3. Now float your head as far to the left as you can and hold it there. Check in with your chin. Make sure it's not tilting up or down.

4. Slowly allow your head to float back to center.

5. Now, turn your head again to the right, keeping the chin level. Once you have turned your head as far right as you can, lift your chin slightly up toward the ceiling until you feel a nice stretch on the upper left side of your neck. Hold.

6. Allow your chin to drop back to a level position and then slowly float it back to center.

7. Let's do the same thing on the left. Float your head to the left. Once you get there tilt your chin up to the ceiling and hold.

8. Allow your chin to come back to a level position and then slowly float it back to center.

Neck Stretches

9. Turn your head one more time as far as you can to the right while still keeping your chin level. This time tilt your chin down at a slight angle until you feel a pull on the left back-side of the neck. Hold.

10. Allow your head to become level and then float it back to center.

11. Turn your head once more to the left, as far as you can. Once you get there tilt your chin slightly down and hold.

12. Allow your chin to become level and float your head back to center.

13. Next, you are going to keep your head facing forward and allow it to tilt to the right. Try to get your right ear to come closer to touching your right shoulder. Hold it.

14. Allow your head to float up to center.

15. Now, let your head tilt to the left shoulder. Keep the head facing forward. Hold.

16. Allow your head to float up to center.

17. Allow your head to roll forward, slowly dropping your chin to your chest and hold.

18. Float your head back to center.

19. Now, I want you to take your right wrist into your left hand behind you and gently pull with your left hand. While you are doing this, I want you to tilt your head to the left. Hold.

20. Float your head back to center while you relax your arms.

21. Switch hands. Take your left wrist into your right hand and gently pull. Tilt your head to the right and hold.

22. Float your head back to center. Release your hands and arms back to your side.

23. And, one last time, slowly drop your head to your chest and hold.

24. Release your head back to center.

Neck Stretches

FOLLOW-UP

Note: *Your neck should feel really loose and relaxed in a supported upright position. This series of neck stretches can be done individually or as a group. The more you do them, the less tension you will carry in your neck and upper shoulder area — the "back-pack" muscles.*

Rest Position

Purposes of the Exercise

To release tension in the neck, jaw, tongue, and base of skull

To project or extend sound

To teach mindfulness

A Brief History of the Exercise:

The content of this exercise is inspired specifically by the Alexander technique and the work I've done with Bonnie Raphael. The form it takes here is, to the best of my knowledge, my own. It was initially developed for use with clients with voice disorders.
— **Kate DeVore**

THE EXERCISE

This exercise is intended to release chronic, habituated tension in muscles that greatly affect phonation and resonance. If we hold these muscles tight all of the time, they tend to stay tight even when we talk. We are creatures of habit. And we can change habit. The first step is awareness.

1. Standing or sitting, without changing anything, mentally "check in" with the muscles at the base of the skull/back of neck. How does that area feel? Notice if there is a shortening/contraction of any of the muscles in that region. Such a tightening might result in your head tilting back a little, or jutting forward. There might simply be a deep holding or bracing of these muscles.

2. If you observe a misalignment or a holding at the base of your skull, ask the questions, "How much can I release this area? How much can I let go?" Observe how this release might move your head in relation to the rest of your body. Release the muscles on the top and front of your spine and in the middle of your head. In this position, the vocal tract is at its natural resting length. There is an acoustic benefit of having this tube open in this way, as opposed to lengthened and distorted with the head protruding.

3. As an experiment, sustain an "ah" sound while moving your head slowly back and forth between the new and old positions, or simply move your head through space — front to back, up and down. Notice that when your head is balanced on your body, your jaw muscles can relax and your voice feels free. Also, as it is common for tension at the back of the body to create a compensatory tension in the front of the body, it is helpful to consciously release tension from the face and front of neck.

Rest Position

4. Now that your head is aligned and the muscles in the back of your neck are released, turn your attention to your jaw. What is your mouth doing? Are you holding any tension in your jaw muscles? Where is your tongue?

5. Keeping your lips gently touching, and release your jaw. Just let it hang easily. There is space between your teeth. Now lay your tongue down and back, like a rug on the floor of your mouth. There is probably a larger space at the back of your mouth than you are used to. Now, maintain that position for a moment.

   If you can separate *mental* effort from *physical* effort, you will see that while this requires a good deal of attention, it is physically easy. That is because this is the natural resting position for the human body. Your jaw is just hanging there. It's important to keep your lips closed because you are reminding your body that releasing tension in the jaw doesn't require a lack of energy in the face.

   This is the rest position: head aligned (through release of tension at the back of the neck), jaw released, tongue released. Shift this position into your consciousness as many times in a day as you can. Whenever you are not using your mouth, bring it into this position. Leave notes around your home and office to remind yourself. Simply check in, observe the current state, release, allow movement, and move on. This doesn't take much time; it takes frequent attention. Over time, the changes you need to make in order to release will probably be increasingly subtle.

6. Keeping your head balanced on top of your body, your jaw relaxed and your tongue flat, say, "mm-hmm." Feel for a vibration of the bone above your upper lip. If you don't feel a vibration, allow even more space in the back of your mouth and do it again. That vibration is the seed of a healthy, resonant mouth.

FOLLOW-UP

Beware the temptation to think, for example, "O.K., I've learned that I carry my head with my chin tilted up, so I need to adjust it downward." While this may be true initially, there is more benefit to organically making the change rather than "putting" your head in the "correct" position. Simply "putting" your head in position can result in new or perpetuated tension, and may also eventually lead to overshooting the target.

Rest Position

As the muscles are repeatedly given permission and encouragement to let go, it is likely that you will carry less habituated tension in these areas and you will need to make a different *adjustment than you do at the beginning of this process.*

This is a process of learning and ongoing awareness. If you learn to be aware of these areas of your body, the tension that instills itself there, and then letting go of it, you will develop a habit of releasing through awareness. *The same is true for the jaw and tongue release.*

Side Stretches at the Barre

Purposes of the Exercise

To stretch the body

To expand breath capacity

To coordinate breath release
with open tone

To release tone with freedom
and rich resonation

To find easy pitch range

A Brief History of the Exercise:

I studied ballet, modern, and jazz dance from the age of six through college. Stretching at the barre was a basic foundation in all three dance genres. When I started exploring voice work as an acting student (at L.A., City College, Carnegie Mellon U., and Wayne State U.) and then as a teacher/coach, I found that variations from dance directly enhanced and solved problems of breath expansion, coordination, and support. I benefited from many dance teachers. I was inspired by voice and speech leaders Robert Parks and Edith Skinner, and mentored ("parented") by Jerry Blunt. This particular exercise is probably an evolution of all these influences, and it continues to evolve with each new student and actor. — **Jan Gist**

THE EXERCISE

Most voice/speech teachers work to expand the rib cage and belly, for expanded breath capacity. I've found that by supporting yourself on the barre, the stretches are more focused on release and less constrained in the effort to lean over. By going through these different positions, a fairly thorough opening occurs. By releasing on easy open glides from high pitch to low, coordination is developed between large breath, full, open tone, and pitch-range confidence.

It is helpful to go through this whole series on both sides of the body and then go into speaking long sentences of text, to apply the breath and tone to thought and intention.

1. Stand at the ballet barre (you can substitute a table or wall; anything strong enough to lean your weight into). Your left side is at the barre. Your left hand is on it. Stand with good, easy alignment, knees unlocked, weight distributed equally between both feet.

2. Reach your right hand and arm up above your head, stretching the right half of your rib cage up and out of the pelvis. Continue to reach up and over to the left side, slightly, enough to really open the right side ribs. You are supporting your weight with your left hand on the barre. Inhale richly and deeply as you stretch, opening the right side and belly vigorously. On the exhale, keep reaching up and over to the left and release an open tone through loose neck, throat, jaw, and tongue. Let the release be an easy open pitch glide from high to low. Repeat in this position two to four times.

3. Lift the sternum and nose towards the ceiling, the right arm slightly up and behind your head, exposing the front of the rib cage and belly by a slight backward arch. (There should be no back strain here. Make sure knees are slightly bent; the arch is about opening the front of the body, not about bending the spine backwards.) Vigorously lift the ribs up and open. Explore the angle of the arm so

Side Stretches at the Barre

that the shoulders are as free as possible, though engaged in the stretch. Inhale fully, taking time to expand the front ribs and belly. Release on an open pitch glide from high to low. Repeat two to four times.

4. Turn to face the barre, both feet pointing toward it. Hold onto it with both hands and drop into a crouch, with knees open. Arms are up, hands are on the barre so both the back and the sides of body are being stretched. (For sore knees, some people may want to sit on the floor here, instead of crouching.) Breathe deeply into the open back, sides, and pelvis. Swing ribs open on both sides equally, then release on an open glide from high to low pitch. Repeat two to four times.

5. Keep your feet on floor. Tilt the tailbone towards the ceiling and hang the torso over the body. Your knees are bent. Let your head hang down freely. Fill with air, chew, and glide pitch up and down as you roll the spine to standing; head is the last to roll up.

6. Return to the left side of the body, place your left hand on the barre, and repeat step #1.

7. Reach your right arm forward diagonally over the barre so that your back is flat and parallel to the floor (you are bent at the hip sockets). The sternum and nose should face the floor. Reach your tailbone away from your head and your right arm away from your tailbone. Open the ribs at the spine and stretch the shoulder blade. Fill with air on the inhale then release by gliding pitch from high to low. Repeat two to four times.

8. Drop the torso over the left knee from the hip sockets. Release both arms, torso, and head over the left knee. Slightly bend both knees. Fill with air, glide pitch from high to low. Repeat two to four times.

9. From here, swing the torso forward so that it hangs over both legs. You are now balanced equally over both feet and knees. Fill with air, glide pitch from high to low. Repeat two to four times. While here, you can hum as you shake the head "no" to loosen the neck. Roll the spine to standing while humming and chewing.

Side Stretches at the Barre

10. Turn to have right side at barre, right hand on the barre, and repeat the whole series on this side.

FOLLOW-UP

This exercise can be done with partners: one doing the exercise, the partner putting his/her hands on the "speaker's" ribs and belly to help him/her feel the potential to fully expand on inhales, and to stay loose and free throughout entire breath cycles in each position.

In the crouch position, other breathing patterns can be explored, such as taking four counts to breathe in, expanding for six more counts, then exhaling from the belly first and then the ribs at the end of the exhale.

Advanced Triangle Pose

Purposes of the Exercise

To stretch the intercostal
    muscles

To connect with breath

To expand breath capacity

A Brief History of the Exercise:

Originally I learned this position as a yoga asana from Bonita Bradley at the American Conservatory Theater in San Francisco in 1976. Over my years of teaching, I have modified it to its current form. — **Nancy Houfek**

THE EXERCISE

This stretch can be done by an individual or in pairs. The following description is for the partnered version.

1. Pick a partner, preferably someone who is roughly your height and weight.

2. Both stand facing the same direction, but not facing each other.

3. Adjust your distance so that your fingertips are touching when your arms are fully extended sideways parallel to the floor.

4. Spread your legs so that your feet are located wider than your shoulders.

5. Turn your toes outward without shifting your hips.

6. With arms extended sideways, parallel to the floor, shift your rib cage toward your partner.

7. Keeping your hips in the same plane as your torso (not letting the hip nearest your partner shift backward), and keeping your legs straight, bring the hand extended toward your partner to your ankle. (If you are less flexible, you may bring your hand to your knee or thigh.)

8. Your other arm should now be pointed toward the ceiling. (This is the traditional Triangle Pose.)

9. Bring the hand that is pointing to the ceiling over your head toward your partner's hand. Take hold of each other's wrists.

10. Gently pull your hips away from your partner, feeling the profound stretch through the intercostal muscles.

Advanced Triangle Pose

11. Breathe fully into the ribs, extending the stretch. Vocalize your sensation rather than holding it in, making sure that your vocalization does not begin with a glottal attack.

12. When you are ready, release your partner's hand and drop forward and hang. Feel the difference in size between the side you just stretched and the side you are going to stretch.

13. Gently shake your shoulders as you roll up the spine.

14. To stretch the other side, both partners turn and face in the opposite direction. Repeat steps 3-13.

Note: *When you have stretched both sides, take a moment to feel how deeply and easily the breath travels into the lungs by having fully stretched the intercostal muscles.*

Balance and Alignment Using the Wall

Purpose of the Exercise
To center the body

A Brief History of the Exercise:
I learned this exercise nine years ago while a student of Bill Pepper, the head of the voice program at the National Institute of Dramatic Art (NIDA) in Sydney, Australia. I have modified it slightly in teaching it over the years by introducing the extension exercises. I have found it to be very valuable to students at the start of their course and have found it to be particularly valuable for corporate clients. They notice an immediate difference. — **Lorraine Merritt**

THE EXERCISE

Pre-Exercise Preparations
I always precede this exercise with a spine roll.

1. Place your heels, buttocks, shoulder blades, and head against the wall.

2. With the placement of the head, check that you do not tilt the chin up or tuck it down. Rather, find the position where the head can rest against the wall and be in the balanced position on top of the spine.

3. Leaving the head resting against the wall, take a generous step away from the wall. Heels, bottom, and shoulders should now be removed from the wall.

4. Place one heel back against the wall.

5. Push away from the wall towards your forward foot and take a walk in the space.

6. Sense the length in your spine as you walk.

7. Sense whether your eye level has shifted from what it is normally. You may feel taller.

Extension 1

1. Do the exercise again.

2. This time, when you are walking in the space, allow your body to return to its normal pattern.

3. Note the difference. Very often, shoulders will drop forward, heads

Balance and
Alignment Using the Wall

will come forward, and spines will collapse, causing a cave-in of the chest and stomach areas.

Extension 2

1. Stand with your feet parallel, about six to eight inches apart.

2. Make sure your weight is evenly distributed over both feet and that your knees are unlocked.

3. Sense the length in your spine and the width in your back.

4. Sense the length in the back of the neck and the head floating on top of the spine.

5. Make sure your jaw is relaxed.

6. Note the movement of the breath in the body.

7. From this balanced, centered position, allow yourself to drift forward until you are off balance, to the point where your toes dig into the floor to stop you from falling over. Note the tension that has entered the body. Check to see if you have stopped breathing.

8. Slowly, allow yourself to drift back to the point of balance. Note the moment when the tension dissolves from the body and the breath deepens in the body.

9. Find the ease in this balanced, released position.

10. Sense the space around your body. Go for a walk, sensing the space around you as you do it.

Twelve-Step Program for Release of Neck, Jaws, and Shoulders

Purpose of the Exercise

To release the face, jaw, sternocleidomastoid, and trapesius muscles

A Brief History of the Exercise:

I created this exercise approximately eight years ago. I was teaching voice classes at George Brown College of Performing Arts in Toronto, Ontario. It seemed that more students than usual in this particular year experienced a great deal of jaw, neck, and shoulder tension. And so this exercise came out of my need to communicate to students (with a sense of humor and yet with great purpose) just how important it is to eliminate tension from these areas in order to access the primary breathing muscles (diaphragm, abdominals, and intercostals) more readily and in turn access a balanced, open, sound quality. — **Susan Stackhouse**

THE EXERCISE   CD: TRACK 1

This is a wonderful exercise to do before drilling speech sounds, eliminating glottal stops, or delivering open, oral sounds. It is done in a sitting position. Ensure that the spine remains aligned, and that you inhale and exhale through the mouth.

1. Place thumbs at the temples and, as you exhale, apply pressure in a circular motion. Release pressure as you inhale. Repeat three times.

2. Move your thumbs down to the jaw hinge. You will find this spot by opening and closing your mouth several times. Apply pressure as you exhale. Release pressure as you inhale. Repeat three times.

3. Move your thumbs down an inch to the lower jaw area and once again apply pressure in a circular motion as you exhale. Release pressure as you inhale. Repeat three times.

4. Place thumbs under the chin on the mandible bone with each thumb approximately one inch from the center. As you exhale through the mouth, apply pressure upwards, bringing the teeth together. As you inhale, let the thumbs fall away and the jaw drop open. Repeat three times.

5. Place thumbs and fingers of both hands on the lower jaw just under the left ear. Upon exhalation, swiftly move along the lower jaw line to the right ear, kneading the muscles and skin. Encourage the jaw to release as you go. Inhale and then move from right to left. Repeat three times.

Twelve-Step Program for
Release of Neck, Jaws, and Shoulders

6. Place the heels of each hand on the jaw hinges. Upon exhalation, encourage the jaw to release using a single, firm massage stroke downward and off the chin. Repeat three times.

7. Gently clasp hands together and, on every out breath, do an up-and-down "shake out" that allows the release to travel up the arms to the face. Repeat three times.

8. With hands still clasped, change to a side-to-side "shake out" that allows the whole body to release. Ensure that the shoulders stay released. Repeat three times.

9. Place the right hand on the back of the neck. Grip the muscles on either side of the spine as if you were picking yourself up by the scruff of the neck. As you exhale, nod the head. Repeat three times.

10. Repeat Step 9 using the left hand. Repeat three times.

11. Throw the right hand across the chest and over the left shoulder. Grab hold of as much of your trapezius muscle as possible. While exhaling, rotate your left shoulder in a circular motion back into the pressure of the right hand and fingers. Maintain pressure throughout this step. Repeat three times.

12. Throw left hand over right shoulder and repeat step eleven. Repeat three times.

Tennis Ball Torture

Purpose of the Exercise

To release the muscles along the spine

A Brief History of the Exercise:

I learned this from Marya Lowry (now teaching at Brandeis University) when I studied at Purdue University. I have not changed it significantly; however, my class did name it the 'Tennis Ball Torture.' — **Phil Timberlake**

THE EXERCISE

Pre-Exercise Preparations:

You will need two tennis balls and a mat.

1. Lie on your back on the mat.

2. Place one tennis ball on either side of your spine, just above the pelvic girdle in the lower back.

3. Relax and release the rest of your body, allowing the tennis balls to give you a deep massage. Leave the tennis balls in place for at least 30 seconds.

4. Moving your body, roll both tennis balls up along the spine, toward your head, about the distance of one vertebra.

5. Relax and release the rest of your body, allowing the tennis balls to give you a deep massage. Leave the tennis balls in place for at least 30 seconds.

6. Continue rolling the tennis balls toward your head, one vertebra at a time, relaxing and releasing the rest of your body, allowing the tennis balls to give you a deep massage.

7. Continue the exercise until the tennis balls reach your upper back, near the neck, where you will no longer feel significant pressure from the tennis balls.

   WARNING: *Do not fall asleep while lying on the tennis balls, as this could cause muscular problems.*

Chapter 3

Breathing and Supporting

Breathing is an automatic process for all of us. However, the professional voice user, whether a speaker, actor, or singer, needs to be able to use the breath to sustain long phrases of thought or a long musical line. This is especially true when the actor is doing classical text—Shakespeare, Shaw, or the Greeks. Sometimes a single sentence of Shakespeare's text contains over 100 words, which must be expressed using breath as the powerhouse behind and under the expression of thought and feeling. It is only when the actor has gained mastery of diaphragmatic or abdominal breathing and is able to engage the abdominal muscles and lower lung lobes fully in breathing that s/he is able to support the text effortlessly. Our goal is to make abdominal breathing a natural part of our everyday life so we don't have to think about it.

The first two exercises of this chapter, Mary Corrigan's "Breath Exercise" (3-1) and "Breath Journal" (3-2), increase our awareness of breath. In gaining access and control over breath it is important for us to make "breath discoveries." Her "Gentle Warm-Up for Breath and Body" (3-3) involves the body and breath in a standing position, while Mary Coy's "Legs on the Chair Breathing Exercise" (3-4) makes us aware of releasing the belly muscles while we are lying on the floor. Each of these four exercises bring us to the awareness of breath while we are in different body positions.

"The "Hey" Breath Exercise" (3-5), created by Ginny Kopf, helps to establish a need to expand breath capacity while energizing the action of breathing. Marya Lowry's "Straw Work" (3-06) uses a drinking straw to help connect awareness of breath and sound to one's primary breath support muscles while establishing the sensation of the forward focus of tone in the mouth. Kate Udall's "Breath Flow" (3-07) returns to a simple connection with breath but adds the kinesthetic element of an arm and hand movement to give outward expression to what is happening internally. This exercise also adds consonant and vowel sounds to simple breathing. Finally, William Weiss's "Awareness in the Sitting Position" (3-08) asks us to observe how we breathe while doing a specific motion with our body and then asks us to change our breathing pattern, thus helping us break out of ingrained breathing patterns.

Breath Exercise

Purpose of the Exercise
To ground and deepen the breath

A Brief History of the Exercise:
Self-originated. — **Mary Corrigan**

THE EXERCISE   CD: TRACK 2

1. Sit comfortably in your chair, with your hands in your lap and your feet on the floor. Allow yourself to relax back into the chair.

2. Become aware of your back resting comfortably against the back of your chair. Experience the weight of your buttocks resting easily on the surface of your chair. Your lips are lightly closed. Your tongue is flat, resting like a spoon inside a bowl. The tip of your tongue is resting behind your bottom front teeth.

3. Breathe in through your nostrils and into your abdomen and back. Let your hands rest lightly on your abdomen. Experience your abdomen moving and filling your hand as air returns. Take another deep breath through your nostrils and again experience your breath in your abdomen and back as your rib cage expands to accommodate your lungs as they fill. Take another deep breath through your nostrils. Become aware of your breath dropping even lower so that you almost begin to feel that you are breathing into your buttocks. Continue to observe your abdomen filling your hand as your inhalation replaces your outgoing breath. Take another deep breath, and experience your feet flat on the floor as you continue to breathe deeply and comfortably.

4. You will begin to feel increasingly "grounded" as you experience your breath dropping into a deeper and deeper part of your body. As you continue to breathe in through your nostrils, you will experience an ever-increasing sense of autonomy and strength.

Breath Exercise

Note: *Students may begin to feel almost as though they are breathing through the soles of their feet (which, of course, is anatomically impossible). I recommend nostril breathing rather than mouth breathing for this exercise only because participants can more readily experience the ribs swinging open to accommodate the incoming breath. But I believe that both forms of breathing are acceptable for voice production.*

Breath Journal

Purpose of the Exercise
To establish awareness of breathing and thought patterns

A Brief History of the Exercise:
Self-originated. — **Mary Corrigan**

THE EXERCISE

1. Begin keeping a "Breath Journal" for three days and nights. Observe the following and record your observations in the journal:

   When do I hold my breath? *(It may seem difficult to become aware of this at first, but most people hold their breath almost all the time.)*

   If you find that you are holding your breath, do two things:

   First, be thrilled that you are becoming aware of your major saboteur of good voice production and a major deterrent to your spontaneous and immediate release of an acting text. (Lack of spontaneity can also get in the way of day-to-day interpersonal relationships!)

   Second, after a day or two of observing your breath patterns (noticing when your breath is unforced and natural and when you hold your breath), begin to analyze those situations that contribute to you holding your breath. Is it when you are auditioning or in angry situations? Or is it when you are on the telephone or when you are fearful and anxious? Or is it simply negative thought patterns that engender your habit of holding your breath?

2. Record those events that contribute to or cause you to "hold your breath." Certain events and/or negative thought patterns may contribute to inadequate breath support.

Note: *Always discuss your breath discoveries in class (if this is a classroom assignment). Breath observations can validate other's similar experiences.*

Gentle Warm-Up for Breath and Body

Purposes of the Exercise

To deepen breath

To improve alignment

To increase body flexibility and enhance sense of empowerment

A Brief History of the Exercise:

This is an exercise that I adapted from a Feldenkrais exercise. — ***Mary Corrigan***

THE EXERCISE   CD: TRACK 3

1. Stand with your arms comfortably crossed at shoulder height, letting your fingertips touch the elbow of the opposite arm. Keep your arms shoulder-height and relaxed. Let the breath drop down into the abdomen.

2. Spray out an "fffff" while letting your entire upper body slowly rotate to the right, keeping your head level with your shoulders. Hold this position until you experience your breath dropping in and down to your abdomen.

3. Now, slowly rotate back to your original position while spraying out an "fffff." Again, experience your breath dropping into your abdomen.

4. Repeat this process, spraying out an "fffff" to your left side. Do this until you experience your breath dropping in.

5. Slowly rotate back to your original position while spraying out an "fffff."

6. Repeat this exercise three times, always waiting for your breath to be replaced. You will probably begin to experience a sense of release before rotating to the next position.

Note: *Participants will find that they can rotate further and further to each side as they repeat the exercise. They should remember to let the head travel with the shoulders to each side and back to the center. Caution participants to keep arms shoulder high and relaxed the entire time! Also, remind them to keep the breath centered and to experience the sprayed "fffff" on the lips.*

Legs on the Chair Breathing Exercise

Purpose of the Exercise

To release the belly muscles

A Brief History of the Exercise:

I learned this exercise in yoga class. It is a nice alternative to lying flat on the floor with legs extended or legs bent at the knees, feet on the floor. In this position you will notice immediate ease of movement in the belly. Over the years, I have used this exercise to help students who have particularly tight abdominal muscles or no sense of a deep breath/belly connection. — **Mary Coy**

THE EXERCISE

1. Lie with your back on the floor, resting your lower legs on a folding chair so that the lower part of the legs are parallel to the floor.

2. Allow your legs to feel heavy on the chair and your hips and lower back to rest heavily on the floor.

3. Notice the movement of the breath in the belly. Let your breath be soft and easy.

4. After a minute or two, maintaining an easy breath and a soft belly, fold your knees into your chest and roll over onto one side into the fetal position.

5. Very easily come up to standing, allowing your belly muscles to continue softening and your breathing to be easy.

The "Hey!" Breath Exercise

Purposes of the Exercise

To connect with breath

To extend breath capacity

To project or extend sound

To strengthen support of the
  voice

A Brief History of the Exercise:

I made up this exercise because I needed something more directly practical and emotional than the basic counting exercise on which it is based. — **Ginny Kopf**

THE EXERCISE

This is a variation on the breath capacity exercise where you count:

1
12
123
1234
12345
123456…

and so on, up to about 15 or 20, taking a quick, deep, silent breath after each line. This counting exercise is excellent for concentrating on the breath, but this new variation puts emotion and meaning into the exercise. Plus, the following exercise is fun and motivates the student to get the message across.

1. Say each line after me. I will be adding words to make the sentence longer and longer, to build up your breath control. Take a quick, deep, silent breath for each line — enough breath to sustain the thought so that the volume will not fade out. This is the pattern:

Say: "Hey!"
    "Hey, I won't!"
    "Hey, I won't let you!"
    "Hey, I won't let you intimidate me!"
    "Hey, I won't let you intimidate me after all!"
    "Hey, I won't let you intimidate me after all I've done!"
    "Hey, I won't let you intimidate me after all I've done for you!"
    "Hey, I won't let you intimidate me after all I've done for you and this company!"
    "Hey, I won't let you intimidate me after all I've done for you and this company, Mr. Smithers!"
    "Hey, I won't let you intimidate me after all I've done for you and this company, Mr. Smithers, so, nyah!"

The "Hey!" Breath Exercise

You may add as many "nyahs" this time as you have breath for, but stop before your throat closes off. So the last time is:

> "Hey, I won't let you intimidate me after all I've done for you and this company, Mr. Smithers, so nyah, nyah, nyah, nyah, nyah, etc."

VARIATION ON THE EXERCISE

2. Follow the same instructions for the exercise above but substitute the following words. Even though the words may seem childish, keep an open throat and don't get whiney.

Say: "Hey!"
"Hey, stop!"
"Hey, stop kicking!"
"Hey, stop kicking my chair!"
"Hey, stop kicking my chair, you nerd!"
"Hey, stop kicking my chair, you nerd, or else!"
"Hey, stop kicking my chair, you nerd, or else I'll tell!"
"Hey, stop kicking my chair, you nerd, or else I'll tell the teacher!"
"Hey, stop kicking my chair, you nerd, or else I'll tell the teacher on you!"
"Hey, stop kicking my chair, you nerd, or else I'll tell the teacher on you, so quit it!"

Then add as many : "quit it"s as you can before running out of breath.

Straw Work

Purposes of the Exercise

To connect with breath

To strengthen support of the voice

To connect sound to supported breath

A Brief History of the Exercise:

Straw work is not new or original. However, this series is one that I developed. I consider it a basic/beginning level exercise, but one that can be returned to at any level. — **Marya Lowry**

THE EXERCISE   CD: TRACK 4

This can be done lying on the floor, sitting in a chair, or standing. If connecting to your abdominal support muscles is new for you, start by lying on the floor, then sitting, and finally standing. You will need a drinking straw for this exercise

1. Place the end of a straw into your mouth and blow out, keeping the breath steadily aimed to a point a few yards in front of you. Blow as if you were blowing out a candle. With one hand on your belly, feel it flatten as your breath goes out. Allow the breath stream to come in through your nose and right down, filling the belly/waist area with movement in the lower back. Immediately blow out the stream of breath again. Establish an easy pattern. Breathe in through the nose into the belly and out through the straw. Continue.

   The point of focus for this practice is connecting the out-breath to the support muscles around and below the waist. Also, you should think of the breath as going out on a steady stream and not letting it drop, as you do with a sigh.

   When you are comfortable with the activity of the abdominal muscles, you can connect sound to the out-breath. At this point, you can begin to let the breath in through your mouth or alternate between mouth and nose.

2. Continue as above adding an "oo." With your lips puckered on the straw, it will sound more like "who." Feel the movement of the abdominal muscles flattening as the "who" goes out through the straw. Again, imagine the sound going out into the room a few yards or more in front of you. Let the breath drop into the belly and go right out through the straw. Continue in a consistent pattern for a series of five to ten breaths. You will feel quite a bit of activity in the abdominal area of your body. You will also feel the sound arriving at your lips, in the front of your mouth. Don't rush the incoming breath.

Straw Work

Pay attention to your head/neck alignment. Adding the sound should not cause you to lead with your chin or collapse the back of your neck.

3. When you are comfortable with Steps 1 and 2 above, continue by changing the pitch on each new breath, going up and down a few half steps.

4. Take the straw away and continue, adding combinations of vowels (e.g., [i], [ei], [æ], [ou], [a]) on the stream of breath. Allow the sound to arrive at the front of the mouth. Feel your abdominal muscles connect and flatten as you speak the vowel phrase. Use the full length of your breath.

5. Finally, add a bit of text. Choose a sonnet or verse piece and use the end of the line as a marker for each new breath. When you are comfortable with the coordination of the exercise, expand to two lines per breath, three, etc. Continue alternating the length of the phrases on a breath stream, e.g., one line/new breath, three lines/new breath, two lines/new breath, four lines/new breath, one line/new breath.

FOLLOW-UP

You have connected breath and sound to your primary support muscles. In addition, you have experienced the breath and sound arriving at the front of your mouth. When you add text (conversation, poetry, song, scripts, etc.), trust that the support is in place and that you do not have to push the sound or intention out of your body, but simply let it ride the supported breath stream.

Breath Flow

Purpose of the Exercise

To connect with breath

A Brief History of the Exercise:

I learned this exercise from David Carey at the Central School. The simplicity of the exercise is very useful for beginners. — **Kate Udall**

THE EXERCISE

1. Stand with your weight balanced and allow breath to flow at your natural rhythm.

2. As your breath releases out, let your hand mirror the flow and duration of your breath. As the breath leaves you, let your hand float away from the body at a comfortable height, about waist/chest high. The action is as if you are opening your arms for a big, one-armed hug. (Think tai chi.) Keep your shoulders released.

3. As you inhale and the breath drops into your body, let your hand fall to your side.

4. And again, as the breath moves out, the hand moves away.

5. Repeat for several minutes. Change arms to avoid fatigue. Let your hand do exactly what the breath is doing. The movement of the arm is no longer or shorter than what is happening physically. You may find that the breath begins to elongate.

6. Continue to let the arm mirror and gently float with the breath. After a few rounds, make the sound "s" as you exhale. Do not attempt to sustain the sound any longer than what is comfortable.

7. Now, make the sound "m" as you exhale. Do not attempt to sustain the sound any longer than what is comfortable. Feel the vibration on your lips, without allowing sound to be caught in the back of your throat.

8. Now, make the sound "maa" as you exhale. Do not attempt to sustain the sound any longer than what is comfortable. Visualize your thought/breath/vibration floating away from you.

Breath Flow

9. Next, take a piece of text and chant it with the arm movement. Let your arm continue to mirror your breath. Chant the text, letting the arm move away from you as you speak and let it fall to your side as the breath drops into the body. Look for a smooth flow of sound/thought, letting your arm and vibration move smoothly in coordination.

10. Then, repeat the piece of text, saying it normally with the arm movement. Use your own natural pitch and intonation.

11. Finally, without the arm movement, speak the piece of text and feel the smooth flow of breath and thought.

Note: *This exercise can really "ease" out the voice and help people find what it is to really speak on the breath. It's very relaxing, too.*

Awareness in the Sitting Position

Purposes of the Exercise
To center the body
To connect with breath

A Brief History of the Exercise:
I created this exercise from an inspiration (followed by an expiration). It is part of the Mobile Voice, Minimal Movements, and Spatialization Method. — **William Weiss**

THE EXERCISE

This exercise, which could also be done standing, is essential for posture. It involves a continuous game with gravity. For the body parts participating in speech to function smoothly, it is important that posture be economical. This exercise facilitates, through awareness, the constant refinement of posture.

1. Sit on a chair, bench, or table.

2. Lean slightly to the right and then let your trunk return to the vertical.

3. Make the movement several times and each time diminish the extent of the leaning, slightly.

4. After a few moments, notice the breathing rhythm accompanying each movement to the right. Do you breathe in? Do you breathe out? Do you hold your breath each time that you lean to the right?

5. Make the movement again, leaning slightly to the right, but this time, invert the breathing pattern. If you breathed in as you leaned to the right, now breathe out as you do it. Conversely, if you breathed out as you leaned to the right, now breath in as you do it.

6. Make the movement several times until it becomes easy for you to stay in a vertical posture.

Note: *Sitting on a table has many advantages since the body is given support all along the thighs, while the lower legs hang down. It is important not to lean on the back of a chair since the trunk should keep the vertical position in relation to gravity. Many Westerners have difficulty sitting on the floor easily in a vertical position and that is why I normally recommend a chair for sitting. In other sessions, do the same exercise in the other directions—toward the left, toward the right, toward the front, and toward the back.*

Chapter 4

Resonating

In the process of phonation, resonating involves the amplification of sound as the sound waves bounce off of the inner tissues and bones of the body. Primary areas of resonance have traditionally been defined as the top of the head, the mask or frontal part of the face (including the nose and sinus cavities), the mouth, the neck, and the chest. Excess tension in any muscle of the body can affect resonance. Try to make a sound while you are tightening the muscles of your neck and the base of the tongue. You will find that when you speak, your voice quality or resonance has changed. Now release the muscular tension and you will hear a sound that is closer to your usual speaking voice.

The exercises in this chapter help us explore our own areas of resonance. All of the exercises involve breath and some involve body movement. Some of the exercises cover a broad spectrum of purposes in addition to the simple exploration of resonance. Eric Armstrong's "Defining the Vowel Space: The Front/Back Glide and Open/Close Slide" (4-1) takes us on a journey through the resonance potential in our own mouths. With this exercise, we are encouraged to create both new and familiar vowel sounds by adjusting the shape of the inside of our mouths. This exercise should be done slowly and quietly. Cynthia Blaise's "Throat and Neck Release on Sound" (4-2) allows us to experience, in gradations, sound mixed with breath to create, finally, a fully resonant sound.

Deena Burke's "Combining Nasal Resonance with Creative Impulse" (4-3) focuses on nasal resonance while Rinda Frye's "Healing Touch" (4-4) is a gentle exploration intended to be used as a warm-up when the vocal range is limited by a cold or the flu. Marya Lowry's "Giving Voice to Your Hunger" (4-5) is intended to be done by a group sitting in a circle or can be done by an individual working alone. It involves giving voice to your own personal sound or finding the soul sound for a character you may be playing. Elizabeth Mayer's "Gliding and Sliding" (4-6) is a wonderful warm-up exercise for opening resonantors and allowing them to respond fully to sound while varying the pitch. Paul Meiers's "To Glottalize or Not to Glottalize" (4-7) addresses ways to minimize and diminish habitual glottal attacking, which can be very damaging to the voice.

In Joan Melton's "The Wailing Routine" (4-8), we contact simple breath, combine breath and movement, and then take all of these into the extended sound of wailing, which wakes up the fullest breathing and sounding. Dorothy Runk Mennen's "Honing the Toning" (4-9) empowers breath and asks us to explore tone by going from soft to loud and then back to soft again. "Hum and Chew — Versions One and Two" (4-10) gently warms up the voice while releasing the jaw hinge. This is a wonderful exercise to do before a performance or speech.

Chapter 4

Mandy Rees's "Improvisation from Primitive Sound" (4-11) is a partner exercise which helps to integrate breath impulse with the exchange of primitive, open sounds between participants. Also a partner exercise, Chuck Ritchie's "Vocal Mirrors" (4-12), which was inspired by Meisner's verbal mirror exercise, encourages sound-based exchanges. Synthesized from the work of Kristen Linklater, Frankie Armstrong, John Wright, and Arthur Lessac, Karen Ryker's "Woo Woe" (4-13) is a quick, lively workout which energizes articulators and engages the voice. Annie Thompson's "The 'Ha'" (4-14) allows a group to focus on body, breath, and space in a communal, joyful way. Phil Timberlake's "Wizard of Oz" (4-15) uses Dorothy's beloved line, "Run, Toto, Run!" and the Wicked Witch of the West's famous line, "Surrender, Dorothy!" to explore skull and head resonators.

Defining the Vowel Space:
The Front/Back Glide and Open/Close Slide

Purposes of the Exercise

To clarify speech

To introduce non-standard
   vowel sounds

To explore vowel modifiers

To experience, hear, and feel
   how vowels are shaped

A Brief History of the Exercise:

I use this exercise to introduce the phonetic concepts of "frontness vs. backness," "opened vs. closed," and "spread vs. rounded." I modified this after reading Peter Ladefoged's A Course in Phonetics. The "stepping" process was something I did a lot of with David Smukler, both while at York University and at Canada's National Voice Intensive. The inclusion of "sliding," as far as I can tell, was my own idea.

— ***Eric Armstrong***

THE EXERCISE

After students have a solid knowledge of all the vowels in English, I introduce the feeling of new vowel sounds, including non-English sounds. I usually use this with a class, but if I have to coach someone learning a dialect on vowel sounds that they have never used, I may quickly use this exercise to help them find the feeling of the vowel.

Pre-Exercise Preparation

Before I begin, I introduce/review the concept of the vowel space — usually by drawing it on the chalk board. Up to this point the vowel space has been pretty theoretical. Here, the students get a chance to connect the concepts with a feeling in their mouths and to gain a greater awareness of the action of shaping vowels. The students should be reminded to keep asking him/herself, "How do I shape vowels?" and, "What makes one vowel different from another?"

The Front-Back Glide

1. On a pitch that is comfortable, intone the vowel sound "EE" [i] (as in "free"). Try to feel the placement of the tongue in your mouth. Imagine the center part of your tongue: Where is it arching? Try to exaggerate this action, so that the sound feels tighter and tighter — your tongue should move closer and closer to the hard palate/alveolar ridge, behind your upper front teeth. At some point the sound will become so closed off that it will no longer be a vowel, but the consonant "y" (as in the first sound in "yes"). Relax this sound back to the "EE."

2. On the same pitch as above, make the sound "OO" [u] (as in "goose"). You will probably feel your lips round forward into a tight, kiss-like shape. However, for this exercise, I want you to focus on the action of the tongue. Try to say OO [u], but with your lips relaxed. Use a small hand mirror to be sure that your lips don't move. Feel where your tongue is in your mouth. You should feel that your tongue has pulled back in the mouth from where it was for the "EE" [i] sound.

Defining the Vowel Space:
The Front/Back Glide and Open/Close Slide

3. To feel this front/back shift more intensely, keep your lips relaxed and let your tongue move in your mouth to go back and forth between "EE" [i] and this new unrounded "OO" [ɯ] sound. You should be able to notice how your tongue isn't merely sliding forward or backward, but the arching action is shifting back and forth through different parts of the tongue in a wave-like motion. Now, try to slow the wave, feeling how the action of the tongue shapes the sound as it glides forward. By keeping the pitch of the sound on the same note, you should be able to hear the overtones shifting higher on the forward sounds, and lower on the backward sounds.

4. Once you have a clear idea of the feeling of this front/back glide, try it with the rounded versions of the vowels. Here we need to learn another non-English vowel, the "u" (as in the French "tu" or German "uber;" [œ] in the IPA). By rounding your lips forward in the "OO" position, then gliding the tongue forward to the "EE" position, *without relaxing or spreading the lips*, you should make this new sound. As in the previous step of this exercise, the only thing that should be moving is your tongue; the lips are frozen in the forward, kiss-like position. Again, use the hand mirror to be sure your lips stay in the kiss position. Focus on the feeling of the wave of the tongue as you block out the lip-rounding sensation. Try to smooth out the action of the wave, so that you're feeling it every step of the way. The sound should be intense. Don't be safe and small with it.

5. Now that you can do the front/back glide, we can explore variations on vowels that might be useful in dialects/accents that you learn in the future. Let's start with the rounded glide, smoothly shifting between "OO" and "u." This time, I'd like you to try to stop the glide at the half way point–when the sound is neither "OO" nor "u."

   Keep gliding back and forth between the extremes, trying to stop on the mid-vowel "ui" as you pass through it. Also, you should try stopping at a point just in front of the "OO" (as in words like "tomb, ooze, use, new.") How would that change the way you speak?

   The sound is represented by the barred-u symbol in the IPA, often spelled as "ui" in Scots words like "guid."

6. Finally, let's try the front/back glide without lip-rounding, stopping at the unrounded closed mid-vowel. Try gliding and stopping at the front, mid, and back places, and feel the action of the tongue as it changes the sound. As you did with the rounded version, you should try stopping just behind the regular "EE" spot. Try using this new

Defining the Vowel Space:
The Front/Back Glide and Open/Close Slide

sound in words that would normally use the regular "EE" (words like "beat, each, reek, team"). What dialect would that sound like?

The IPA represents this with a barred, lowercase i. This reduced version of EE [i] is often heard in unstressed syllables at the ends of words in some English variants, e.g., in the final syllable of words like "pretty." It is neither the open i [I] sound of "this" nor the further forward sound of EE [i].

The Front Open/Close Slide

1. We are going to work on how the vowels made in the front of the mouth share the front quality we discovered in the front/back slide above, while noticing the differences between each vowel. This difference is made primarily by the tongue or jaw. To feel this in a big way, start by going back and forth between "EE" and "a" (as in the word "trap"). You probably feel your jaw doing a lot of work, opening your mouth to the "a" place. However, we can make the shift between both sounds with just our tongues. Start in the open place you found for the vowel "a" (as in the word, "trap"). Keeping your jaw dropped, that is, using only your tongue, make the "EE" sound. As you can feel, we don't need to close our mouths to make the "EE" sound; we need to get the arch of the tongue close enough to the hard palate and alveolar ridge. We can do that with the jaw, or with just the action of the tongue. For this exercise, we will focus on the tongue, so that we can feel its action clearly.

2. On a pitch that is comfortable, begin with the vowel sound "EE." We will now "step down" through all of the vowels made in the front of the mouth. The first step is a small one, to the vowel "i" ([I], as in "this"). Go back and forth between the two vowels, hearing the difference in the sound and sensing the action of your tongue. (You might notice that your tongue pulls back slightly on the "i" sound. Technically, this sound is made more centrally than all the other "front" vowels. Can you feel the portion of your tongue that is moving?

3. Now, we will add a vowel to our set of steps —"A" [e] (as in the word, "gate," or at the end of the French word "café," or in the first half of the diphthong AY [eI], as in "face"). It is important that you make this sound a pure "A" [e] sound and not the diphthong, as that shift will send us back up toward the top of the stairs! So, starting at EE [i], step through "I" [i] to "A" [e] and then back up the steps through "i" [I] to "EE" [i]. People often find that climbing back up the steps is far more difficult than stepping down. Work through

Defining the Vowel Space:
The Front/Back Glide and Open/Close Slide

these sounds slowly at first, and gradually pick up speed, keeping each step solid and consistent. Throughout this exercise, try to keep the slide happening on the same pitch. If you let the pitch slide down as your tongue moves down, it is harder to hear the changes in the vowel quality above the change in pitch.

4. Once you can do that with confidence, you can add the vowel sound "e" [ɛ] (as in "dress"). Step through all the vowels we have done so far and then return back up to the "EE" [i]. Focus on the sensation of your tongue, keeping the jaw immobile. You may need to use your fingers on your jaw to keep it still at first. As you learn to isolate the tongue from the jaw, you will no longer need those helping hands.

5. The next sound to add (which makes five vowel steps so far) is the sound we used to contrast the action of the tongue and jaw in step 1—"a" [æ]. Start with "EE" [i], work your way down each step to "a" [ae] and then back up. Is it getting any easier? You should be able to feel the tongue dropping down in your mouth, with the tip of your tongue quite still behind your lower-front teeth. Remember not to let the pitch shift, so you can listen for the quality of sound that is changing while the note stays the same.

6. The final sound in the front open/close step series is "ah" [a]. This vowel is used by some North American speakers in words like "bath" ("ask-list" words, for those familiar with the work of Edith Skinner) and is the first sound in the diphthong "I" [aI] (as in "time"). For those unfamiliar with the sound, the following may be one of the easiest ways to work on it.

Start in the "a" [æ] place, and try to move your tongue further down in the same direction as it was traveling from the steps above. It may feel like the portion of your tongue that has been lowering is pressing itself into the bottom of your mouth. However, be sure that you aren't allowing your tongue to move backward in your mouth. This will create another vowel altogether and defeat the purpose of this exercise. Once you know which sound you are striving for, try stepping down and up through the entire sequence:

"EE" [i] – "I" [I] – "A" [e] – "e" [ɛ]– "a" [æ] – "ah" [a] – "a" [ae] – "e" [ɛ]– "A" [e] – "I" [I] – "EE" [i]

Defining the Vowel Space:
The Front/Back Glide and Open/Close Slide

Taking your time to really clarify each sound helps solidify the action of your tongue in your mouth. Work slowly and carefully at first, and then try to pick up the pace. There are a lot of sounds to remember in this sequence. If looking at the text helps, follow along with your finger so you don't get lost.

7. Now that you can step your way through this action, we must now shift the action of the tongue into the "slide" for which this exercise is made. Start with the "EE" [i] sound again, but try to slide through *all* the sounds, as if your staircase were now a slope down which you were sliding. You should feel yourself pass through each "checkpoint" that we did above, but never stop at them. I find that it helps to follow along with my finger to remind me where I'm headed while also making sure that I'm sliding past each checkpoint without a pause. Go slowly to avoid your natural inclination to stop on one of the steps.

8. You can use this front open/close slide to help you discover how to make vowels that are made in a different manner than the ones you usually say. For instance, you might want to learn how to make "e" [ɛ] (as in "dress") sound more closed without it becoming "A" [e] (as in "gate"). By sliding between the two, you can stop at the halfway point, or just a little bit more closed than "e" [ɛ] or slightly more open than "A" [e]. This is an essential skill to learning complicated dialects.

The Back Open/Close Slide

1. This exercise is a mirror image of the front open/close slide, so I will merely detail the vowel steps one must pass through while stepping and then sliding. However, it should be noted that in the closed position where we start on the sound "OO" [u], it is very difficult to isolate the jaw from the action of lip rounding necessary. In the front open/close slide, we could focus merely on the tongue, but here we must try to feel its action while being conscious of the action of the jaw and lips as well. Many of the sounds in the back open/close slide may be unfamiliar to North American speakers, as the final three sounds may be amalgamated into a single sound in their usage. Hopefully, this process will help those speakers learn these new sounds and to clarify their differences.

2. Let me start by giving you a chart of the vowels in the back open/close slide:

   "OO" [u] – "oo" [U] – "O" [o] – "Aw" [ɔ]– "o" [ɒ] – "AA" [a] – "o" [ɒ] – "Aw" [ɔ] – "O" [o] – "oo" [U] – "OO" [u]

Defining the Vowel Space:
The Front/Back Glide and Open/Close Slide

We begin with "OO" [u] (as in "goose") and step back and forth with "oo" [ʊ](as in "foot"). You may find that "oo" [ʊ] is similar to "I" [I], in that it is more central than the other sounds in the back open/close slide.

The third sound is O [o], a pure "o" sound, which one might recognize from a Scots dialect version of the word "OATmeal"–it's the first element of the diphthong "Oh" [Oʊ] (as in "goat"). The fourth sound is the open "o," Aw [ɔ] (as in "thong"). This sound is unfamiliar to many North American speakers, and can be made by keeping the lips firmly rounded forward, opening the mouth further than on the pure "o." You should feel your cheeks mildly hollow. The fifth sound is the short "o," [ɒ], as in "hot" or "honest." Here the mouth should be quite open, but still slightly rounded. The final sound is different from all the vowels that precede it in the back open/close slide, in that it has no rounding whatsoever. This is the sound "AA" [a] (as in "father").

3. Once you can say each vowel confidently, begin the additive process of going between one vowel and the next, stepping through until you can go through the whole sequence in the chart above. Your attention should be on the feeling of the tongue and how the rounding begins to taper off as we approach the final two vowels in the sequence downward. As with the front open/close slide, you now must begin to slide through the sounds as if you were slipping down a slope rather than climbing down a ladder. Feel the action of lips, tongue, and jaw together. Then repeat the slide, focusing on the feeling of just the lips, or tongue or jaw. Try modifying the slide by limiting the amount of lip rounding you use, then by exaggerating that amount. Do the same limiting/exaggerating process with the jaw. How little can you use your jaw? How much?

FOLLOW-UP

Now that you have done these slides, you should have a better idea of what is meant by the idea of "frontness vs. backness," "opened vs. closed," and "spread vs. rounded." You could try making front/back glides at any point–say gliding back and forth from" ah" [a] to "AA" [a], or from "A" [e] to an unrounded version of "O" [o].

Throat and Neck Release on Sound

Purpose of the Exercise
To relax the throat and neck and create sound without tension.

A Brief History of the Exercise:
This is an exercise I designed to help students stop the throat tightening habit.
— **Cynthia Blaise**

THE EXERCISE   **CD: TRACK 5**

1. Start lying down or in the supine position, if you like. Take a few minutes to establish awareness of abdominal support. If there is time to significantly deepen the breathing, then you can also reinforce the use of rib swing, the simultaneous expansion of ribs and diaphragm, and abdominal support.

   Align the spine using the support of the floor and be sure to release the hips and shoulders. Release the back, especially between the shoulder blades. Frequently turn the head from side to side. Bring the head to center and make small circles with the nose to make sure that the neck is free. All breathing takes place through the mouth. Avoid jaw tension. Keep the tip of the tongue gently resting behind the lower front teeth. Allow all facial tension to leave the face.

   With a hand on the belly, establish the image that the hand guides and monitors the deep lower abdominal muscles in support of the outgoing breath. Place your other hand on your throat, and make sure that the throat and neck remain free of strain and tension. At this point, the outgoing breath should be breath only — no vibrations.

2. Now, at a comfortable pitch, add approximately 10% vibration to the outgoing breath, using as little sound as possible. You should feel no tightening in the throat — none whatsoever, either in the hand or inside the neck area. The sound may be barely audible, and that's just fine. Explore this sensation of a complete lack of throat tension for a few minutes.

3. Now change the mix to 80% breath and 20% vibrations. Again, with one hand on the throat and the other on the belly, monitor the freedom in the neck. There should be no tension. Move to a mix of 70% breath and 30% vibration. Reinforce the abdominal support. The

Throat and Neck Release on Sound

abdomen is the only part of the body that does any work.

4. Move on to 60% breath and 40% vibrations. The minute you sense tension, go back to the last mix of breath and vibration where your throat felt completely free. From this point, gingerly add vibration until you can build up to the next increment with complete freedom.

5. Go forward from here. Keep working until you have integrated roughly 90% vibration with 10% breath without any tightening, squeezing, coercing, holding, pushing, or forcing in the throat area.

Notes: *All work should be done in the student's keynote range.*

Add pitch variation as another layer later on.

Work on projection gradually while carefully monitoring the throat for tension and the belly for support.

Move on to gibberish and then on to calm phrases.

After calm phrases, attempt vocally demanding ones and gradually heighten the dynamics until they can be spoken with as little throat tension as possible.

When success is accomplished on the floor, have the student repeat the exercise in a standing position.

The student will probably never be entirely tension free, especially on very dramatic lines, but s/he can usually release a great deal of the tension s/he thinks of as "good acting."

Until a student knows what throat tension feels like, and what it feels like to produce a free sound, s/he cannot begin to replace the old habit with the new.

Combining Nasal Resonance with the Creative Impulse

Purposes of the Exercise

To connect with breath

To connect the breath to nasal resonance

To connect nasal resonance with the "creative" impulse (an acting impulse or intention)

To begin to combine/assimilate the creative or acting impulse with voice work

To strengthen support of the voice

To use language and speech sounds in the pursuit of an objective

To help free the voice

To help place the voice (find a specific focal point)

A Brief History of the Exercise:

I learned this exercise at the Juilliard School from Liz Smith, a wonderful voice teacher. At that time, I understood it only as an exercise to increase awareness and to use nasal resonance as a way of freeing the voice. As I began to teach, I became aware of a separation that students make between the acting process and what they consider to be "technical" elements of training. I feel it is very important to begin connecting the two early on. When these elements are separated for too long, the actor ceases to discover how intertwined they truly are and how one element informs the other. To that end, I ask students to combine the work they are doing in their acting class with the voice work—even in what might seem like "silly" exercises.

— **Deena Burke**

THE EXERCISE

In class I would first choose a phrase that we would all work on together before having the students choose one of their own. For example: "Alone, alone, all, all alone, alone on a wide, wide sea … " (For suggestions of phrases, please see the end of the exercise description.) I would develop a "story" to give the students a sense of what I was after, i.e., high stakes, specificity, clear given circumstances. I would also introduce this exercise after some exploration of nasal resonance has already occurred. It shouldn't be the first nasal resonance exercise that we work on.

1. Choose one of the phrases that you particularly like. Let it be one that stimulates your imagination and that you can endow with clear given circumstances. Choose one around which you can invent a good story.

2. Take some time (this can be a homework assignment) to create vivid given circumstances. Choose a high stakes scenario. Make up circumstances that compel you to say these exact words. Dare to be dramatic, even overly dramatic, but you must take your story completely seriously. It must be very detailed. Humor is O.K., too — as long as the story has high stakes and you completely invest in your very specific givens.

3. Spend some time playing with just the sounds in the phrase. Stay on the voice. Pay particular attention to the nasal consonant sounds. Enjoy them. Feel the vibrations in the "mask" (the nose, cheeks, lips, etc.). Exaggerate them. Taste them. Ponder how you might use them to help communicate the intention of your phrase determined by your specific scenario.

4. Begin to fully imagine your "scenario." Where are you? What are you wearing? Are you alone? If not, who is with you? What is your relationship with this person? Is there something different about the

Combining Nasal Resonance with the Creative Impulse

relationship today? If so, why? What has happened, specifically? What is the weather like? Are you indoors or out? What does the room, garden, ship, deck, etc., look like specifically? What direction is the wind blowing from? Can you feel it on your clothes, skin? What happened that brought you to this moment and causes you to need to speak these words? Fully justify these reasons and this need.

5. Let your story lead you to your physical position in the space — sit, lie, stand, etc. Set the space with chairs, props, and whatever you need to fully invest in the specifics you've developed. Just as you would in the situation, move around as you use your phrase to communicate the story. *I always encourage students to use other classmates if they wish, providing that a real person may help them invest more fully in the situation. The partner should know what the scenario is and should be silent.*

6. Begin to speak your phrase, remaining fully engaged in the givens of your story. Feel free of the burden to plan it, or make it "be" a certain way. Take a journey with your story and phrase.

7. Can you use the consonant sounds to help intensify your scenario, intensify your intention? Try making the consonants even longer. Explore elongating vowel sounds or shortening them. *If the students know the International Phonetic Alphabet and rules of vowel length, I encourage them to use those as the basis for their long and short explorations.* Be sure to stay completely on the voice. Use and enjoy the vibration and sensation of the nasal resonance. Avoid whispering for intensity. Instead, use the consonants for that.

Notes: *I generally begin with all of the students spread out around the room working on their own, but simultaneously. I give them time to play, following the guidelines above. I listen and am available to answer questions and give input. Eventually, I have them get up one by one and do the exercise while the other students observe.*

The teacher can also side-coach by encouraging the student to a more committed exploration, or by asking specific questions about the scenario, helping the student to make stronger, more specific, higher stake choices before having them do it again.

After each presentation, allow time for comments and observations both from the observing students and the student who did the exercise. Encourage the students to make all comments as detailed and specific as the scenarios were required to be.

Combining Nasal Resonance with the Creative Impulse

LIST OF SUGGESTED PHRASES

1. Many moaning men — many, many moaning men.
2. Come away, come away, come.
3. Make room, make room — the king!
4. We climbed and climbed.
5. A mermaid sitting upon a stone, combing and combing her long green hair.
6. My mind is my own.
7. Miles and miles of golden sand, meandering in a lazy motion.
8. "A drum, a drum; Macbeth doth come."
9. Glimmer, glimmer, glitter, gleam.
10. Marry me, marry me, marry me!
11. Calm and smooth as music murmuring.
12. Somewhere, sometime ...
13. On and on and on.
14. The madman moans at the moon.
15. One, and only one.
16. The psalm is sung — the night is calm.
17. Only the sound of the lonely loon.
18. Wandering and wondering, I went my way around the river bend.
19. I'm alone again — alone, alone, alone
20. Alone, alone, all, all alone, alone on a wide, wide sea ...
21. Mine is the blame. Mine, mine.
22. "Mother, give me the sun."
23. "What's done is done, and cannot be undone."
24. The mournful whistle of the night train.
25. No moon, no sun ... none, none.
26. Nothing, nothing, nothing.
27. The bells bang and clang — ding-dong, ding-dong, ding-dong.
28. Waltzing together the whole night long. Gliding and floating on wings of song.
29. She was hopping and bobbing and skipping along.
30. The bird's on the wing. It's spring, it's spring.
31. He's wrong, he's wrong.
32. Sing out, sing out — sing!
33. Watching and waiting.
34. Swinging and flinging it down.
35. Hanging around with the gang.
36. Moaning and groaning.
37. Number one, number seven, number nine, number ten, number eleven, number nineteen, number ninety-nine.

Healing Touch

Purpose of the Exercise

To open resonance and gently explore range in a voice which has been limited by a cold or flu

A Brief History of the Exercise:

This exercise is my creation, but its inspiration was a partnered vocal exploration I learned from Kristin Linklater (herself inspired by her encounter with Reiki touch some ten or twelve years ago). — **Rinda Frye**

THE EXERCISE   CD: TRACK 6

A word of caution: This is not a substitute for rest, sleep, medication, or a doctor's care. Nor will it give you back your full vocal range when your voice is hoarse or limited by a sore throat. But when you absolutely must perform with a sore throat and a weak or limited voice, this exercise will help you to find and open what limited voice you have, with minimal pain. Remember, work gently. Pay close attention to what your body is telling you, and back off if you feel pain.

1. Find a comfortable position with your head balanced easily on top of an elongated spine and neck. You can do this exercise either lying down, with your knees up and feet on the floor, or sitting in a chair with a flat, firm bottom, your feet easily apart and flat on the floor.

2. Close your eyes and scan through your body, letting your mind move to your center, just behind and below your navel. Gently place both hands on your belly, covering as much of it as you possibly can. Let your hands and arms relax. Feel your hands begin to soften and warm the muscles beneath them.

   Let your lips part and allow the breath to drop deep within the bowl of your pelvis and then release freely over the lips. On the next breath, let the belly soften and release the inside of the hip sockets. (If you find that cold air coming in directly through the mouth causes coughing, close the lips and breathe through your nose. Take care to release the tongue so that the tip falls easily behind the bottom teeth and the center of the tongue relaxes into the floor of the mouth.)

   Picture a huge space available to you in the pelvis, just beneath your hands, from hip bone to hip bone in the front, from the front of the belly to the sacrum and buttocks at the back, and across the floor of the pelvis between your legs. Allow all of these areas to be moved by the breath. As these muscles ease and soften, imagine that the incoming breath is filling this internal space with a golden light. Drop

Healing Touch

the thought of a sigh of relief into the pelvis and sigh out on air alone. Let the breath replace, then drop the thought of another sigh into the pelvis, this time on a relaxed sound, from the lowest note of your register. As you sigh out, let the lips close so that the sigh releases as a deep, rumbling hum. Picture the golden light of the pelvis filling the vibrations of the sigh/hum. Try this sigh/hum two or three times. If you feel little or no pain, try another sigh on this same low note through an open mouth.

3. Release your hands from your belly and gently place them across your upper chest, covering as much of the upper rib cage as possible. Again, let the hands soften and warm the muscles and bones of your chest cavity. Picture the hugeness of the chest cavity with the vaulted arches of the rib cage and all the spaces available for breath and resonance from the distance between your two hands and the space between your hands and the floor. Picture that space filling with air and golden light as the muscles and bones soften, melt, and ease with the warmth. Drop the thought of an unvoiced sigh into the pelvis. Imagine it releasing through the vast space of your chest cavity, out over your lips and into the air. Imagine that the space under your hands could fill with vibrations. Let those vibrations become a color, maybe a rich hazelnut brown. Drop the impulse for a new sigh into the pelvis. This time release the vibrations in the chest a halftone higher than the last voiced sigh. Again, close the lips as you release a low rumbling sigh/hum. Try this again, opening the lips at the end of the hum for an open-mouthed sigh. Repeat this process three or four times, using these same images, but sighing a halftone higher each time, first on a sigh/hum, then on a sigh/hum/full sigh. If your voice hurts, drop back down a halftone and explore the range you've already found.

4. Continue this same process of gentle exploration while cupping the front of the throat and the back of the neck with your hands. Let your hands warm your throat without resting their weight against it. Picture the space in the throat opening and softening, and also picture the spaces between each of the seven vertebrae in your neck. As you begin to sigh, you may only explore one or two notes in this area, starting with the last tone you explored in the chest cavity and moving only a halftone upward at a time. You might explore changing the color of the sighs from this area, or you might keep them within the gold and brown range.

5. Finally, cover as much of the face, jaw, and sinuses as possible with your hands. Let the warmth of your hands ease and soften these areas while you visualize the space available for air and vibrations.

Healing Touch

When focusing on the face, pay particular attention to softening the inside of the mouth so that the tip of the tongue touches the bottom teeth and the center of the tongue drops into the floor of the mouth. Picture the space at the back of the mouth and throat with the soft pallet opening upward. Visualize the double dome of the hard palate with its own arches. Feel the jaw muscles soften under your hands. Picture space and golden air filling the nasal passages and sinus cavities in the cheekbones on either side of the nose and between the eyes. As you sigh into and through all of these spaces, first on breath and then on voice, explore the resonance of each of these areas by incremental halftones, changing your images of colors as you work. Again, drop your range if you feel pain or discomfort.

FOLLOW-UP

This exercise might easily replace your usual vocal warm-up. You should allow yourself plenty of time to warm those sore vocal folds — maybe an hour or more before curtain. And you might consider continuing this whenever you're offstage, while sitting in the wings or in the dressing room.

Giving Voice to Your Hunger

Purposes of the Exercise

To expand the actor's sound imagination and vocal expressiveness

To open pathways to primal, deeply felt, human sounds

A Brief History of the Exercise:

I developed this with my students. — ***Marya Lowry***

THE EXERCISE

This exercise is done with a group sitting around in a circle. It can also be done as solo work.

1. Think of something you "hunger" for — a very strong need, deep desire, a longing.

2. Be specific.

3. Take your time.

4. Now, one at a time and whenever you are ready, "give voice" to the deeply personal sound that expresses your hunger.

   Instruct the students to try to hit it right away. Instruct them not to work up to it. If, however, they are not satisfied that the sound matched the "hunger" as they imagined it, encourage them to repeat it until they feel they have expressed it. Because it is their sound, they are the judge of whether or not they vocally expressed what they imagined. They are not to think of a sound which expresses the hunger, but rather, simply express the hunger through the sound. It is a subtle, but profound difference.

   Each person "gives voice" when they are ready. Allow time for silence and for the group to receive each sound before going on to the next person. Witnessing is an important aspect of this experience. This is not a "head" sound; that is, decided intellectually and then voiced. If time is taken, the actor will find his/her way to the visceral sound. While it may provoke emotions, that is not the intention. The kinds of sounds expressed are usually primal and vulnerable but not necessarily big or extravagant. It is a risky venture, builds ensemble, empathy, and expands the actor's courage to express the inner self with sounds not often heard in public. It can be built upon and opened up to many directions.

Giving Voice to Your Hunger

VARIATION ON THE EXERCISE

Applying the exercise to text.

1. Choose a word that describes the character's primary need in a scene.

2. Reflect for a moment on the impulses that are stirred up.

3. Give voice to the need. Create one sound for one very specific need/hunger.

Note: *This application may reveal the primal hidden beneath language and can provide a way to personalize the text. It can, of course, be done for larger or smaller segments of a play. Once they get over the initial insecurity of revealing the hidden truths of their souls, actors love this exploration.*

Gliding and Sliding

Purposes of the Exercise

To warm up the voice

To connect the voice with
   breath, tongue, and
   soft palate

To open resonators

A Brief History of the Exercise:

The first two parts of this exercise I put together from a vocal re-education I had with Dr. Benoit de la Breteque, a wonderful "phoniatre" (voice doctor) in France. I learned the [ng] slide (called "glissade" in French) directly from him. — ***Elizabeth Mayer***

THE EXERCISE

1. Standing with the knees relaxed, let the breath drop in through the mouth while relaxing the lower belly and opening the ribs. This is the kind of breath you take in when you have a nice surprise! Now let the breath out easily on an [s → z]. The diaphram rises gently, and you can feel a slip of air coming out of the mouth and onto the palm of your hand. Repeat this several times, giving the breathing process and the body plenty of time. The [s → z], of course, engages the tongue.

2. Women begin around middle C, D, or E (or on a comfortable pitch if no piano is available), and men start an octave or so below. Now, sing/speak the word "sing," down a fifth, note by note, i.e., you're singing/speaking "sing, sing, sing, sing, sing." Repeat this series from the next note up, going up to a third or fifth (or sixth...) from the original starting note. Stay within a comfortable range and always let the breath drop into a relaxed lower belly while opening the ribs. Why the descent? Because it's easier. And this is a warming up exercise.

3. Go back to the starting note and let the voice slide down a third, evenly, on the slightly lengthened "n ng" sound, (i.e. the last part of the word "sing"). Let out a short, easy thread of air through the nose before adding the "n ng" sound. (With the "nng" sound, the back of the tongue is on the soft palate and air can't come through the mouth–the "n ng" is on the air.) Repeat the "n ng" slide from the next note up, and the next, going (as before) up a third or fifth or sixth from the original starting note.

4. Finally, go back to the starting note and sing/slide the "n ng" up and down a third. Repeat this sing/slide on the next note up, and on, for a third, fourth, fifth, and so on. Repeat this process with sung/slides going up a fifth and, if this is comfortable, going up and down a sixth, and then an octave. Always let the breath drop in easily, open

Gliding and Sliding

the ribs, let out a thread of air first, and think in terms of circles, rather than simply going up and down the scale.

Notes: *I'd like to add some quotes from Patricia Palamara, a wonderful singer and teacher here in France. She imparted these pearls of wisdom to me during singing lessons, and I have found them to be really helpful, both for myself and for other people, too.*

"Air is everywhere ... it's like water and goes into whatever space is there to receive it. When you breathe in, the body opens...You don't need to 'take' air in, or stretch your neck out, or do anything desperate or hasty. You do need to let the lower belly drop down, and open the ribs... Prepare the body.

"The body, and that includes the mouth (buccal cavity), is an auditorium, and the air turns inside the (open) mouth like a fountain. Sound is created inside and you don't need to push, pull, hold, press anything to 'make sound' ...

"Remember the nape of the neck. It needs to be open, as if you have an open mouth there — and on the sternum, the diaphragm, the sacrum. When you're singing you might just think of the body as a bunch of open mouths...!"

To Glottalize or Not to Glottalize

Purpose of the Exercise

To help overcome the habitual and unconscious use of glottal stops

A Brief History of the Exercise:

I developed this exercise some years ago after observing that some actors seem addicted to glottally attacking all vowel-initial words, producing an invariable staccato rhythm. (This rhythm is dominant in the now ubiquitous "mall-speak".) While glottally stroking a key word that happens to begin with a vowel can be a good choice, serving to isolate a word or clarify a difficult phrase, I wanted to help actors overcome the habitual and unconscious use of glottal stops. Of all the tools of emphasis (pitch, duration, volume, glottal attack, etc.) glottal attack seems the crudest. It is also potentially damaging to the vocal cords. — **Paul Meier**

THE EXERCISE

1. "All Americans Eat Every Ounce of Avocado Available"

Every word in the above sentence begins with a vowel.

    a. Completely staccato (glottally attacking each word).

    b. Completely legato (no glottals).

    c. Legato except for "every ounce" — glottally strike each of those two words lightly.

    d. Legato except for "Americans" — glottally strike that word lightly.

    e. Completely legato (no glottals) — but with strong emphasis on "Americans," "every," and "ounce." Notice that the strong emphasis is achieved with pitch, intonation, and duration.

2. Experiment with other combinations of pitch, duration, intonation pattern, volume, glottal stops, etc., to vary the rhythm and the strategies that you employ for emphasis.

3. Finally, apply these techniques to the following Shakespeare text (vowel-initial words are in bold italics):

> *How happy some **o'er other** some can be!*
> *Through **Athens I am** thought as fair as she;*
> *But what **of** that? Demetrius thinks not so;*
> *He will not know what **all** but he do know;*
> ***And** as he **errs**, doting **on** Hermia's **eyes**,*
> *So **I admiring of** his qualities.*

> — Shakespeare, *A Midsummer Night's Dream*, I, i

To Glottalize or Not to Glottalize

Speak the passage in the following styles:

    a. Completely staccato.

    b. Completely legato.

    c. Legato except for a few carefully chosen words (e.g., o'er, other, errs, I).

4. Experiment with the different strategies for emphasis, creating different rhythms and phrasing patterns.

Note: *Both for the ear of the listener and the throat of the speaker, actors should have control over glottal stops, using this effective (but potentially harmful) plosive only when needed, avoiding its excessive and unconscious use. In this way actors will have equal facility in both legato and staccato styles.*

The Wailing Routine

Purposes of the Exercise

To stretch intercostal muscles

To connect with breath

To extend pitch range

A Brief History of the Exercise:

I developed the exercise for students of Arts Education during my teaching practice.
— **Joan Melton**

THE EXERCISE

Keep both sit bones on the floor throughout this exercise.

1. Sit cross-legged on the floor, balanced on the sit bones. Curl back the upper body, feeling a stretch in the neck and across the shoulders as you allow breath to drop in. Return to an upright position as you exhale. Repeat.

2. Stretch out and up with the arms as breath drops in. With your hands clasped, press up as you exhale. Pull back gently with the arms (hands should remain clasped together) as breath drops in — the breath should feel as if it is dropping into the belly. Exhale and extend the body over the legs, hands still together, arms stretching gently. Reach the arms towards the floor as breath drops in — the breath should feel like it is dropping into the buttocks. Exhale and move to standing. Hands should remain together until you are upright. Release the hands and open to your starting position with a long exhalation.

3. Loosen the shoulders, release the jaw, and gently move the head. Swivel the upper body from side to side, with the elbows bent.

Note: *This is a great place to insert some articulation work.*

4. There are four parts to this final step of the exercise.

   a. Move back to a sitting position. Stretch one leg straight and out to the side, while keeping the other leg bent. Turn the torso toward the leg that's out, check forward movement from the tailbone. Do not round the back, even if the movement is very slight.

   b. The arm opposite the leg that is out swoops down with a good follow-through. Do this four times and blow breath out on each swoop.

The Wailing Routine

    c. Then the arm swoops down, curves up, out and over the ground. Support your weight as the other arm extends up and overhead, stretching and opening the chest, four times. Now, "wail" with the mouth open by saying "AH." Move from a high to low pitch sound — a glissando.

    d. Finally, and only once, do the same action with the arm, and as you bring the other arm up and overhead, go up on the knee that is bent. Allow breath to drop in, then "wail" from a low to high pitch as you come back to the ground and round the body over the outstretched leg. Change sides and repeat.

5. End this entire set of exercises with a cat stretch or crouch.

Note: *The last part of the exercise is very rhythmic and feels like four beats per bar, i.e., on (1), each swoop is a beat; on (2), the beats are: swoop, move, land, return; and on (3), swoop, move, land, breathe, move, and curve (two full measures). These are side stretches, so do not twist to the back at any time.*

Honing the Toning

Purposes of the Exercise

To develop the ability to begin a tone softly and let it grow to loud, then return from loud to soft

To learn to control the breath pressure as one moves from soft to loud and returns from loud to soft

To help develop an "even scale"

A Brief History of the Exercise:

This exercise was developed from the bel canto style of singing of the 18th century. William Vennard uses it in a developed form in his text for singing, Singing: The Mechanism and the Technique.* *I have modified it and continually do so, depending upon my students and their individual needs. This exercise benefits both the speaking and singing voice.* — **Dorothy Runk Mennen**

* *Vennard, William.* Singing: The Mechanism and the Technique. *(New York: Carl Fischer. 1967).*

THE EXERCISE

Note: Steps 1 through 5 are important preparatory steps.

1. Prepare by stretching, yawning, and shaking.

2. Do a yawn while engaging the whole body.

3. Look in the mirror

   a. Do you see a nice oval shape to your mouth?

   b. Do you feel an open throat?

   c. Is the tongue lying loosely on the floor of your mouth?

4. Do several Yawn-Sighs and move about the room freely. (A Yawn-Sigh is a full yawn, then a sigh out from the top pitch to the bottom pitch of your voice.)

5. Follow these with "glissandos." (Singing the top note and gliding down easily to the lowest note. Cover every semitone as you glide down.) Now you should be warmed up for this exercise.

6. Assume a good standing position.

7. Choose a comfortable note in your range.

8. Inhale and begin the note easily and quietly with [a]. (If another vowel is easier for you, do that first.) If you have trouble, begin with an imaginary "H" in front of the vowel.

9. Let the tone grow from soft to loud on the same pitch. Then let it become soft again.

Honing the Toning

10. Repeat until you feel, or your partner or teacher feels, that you understand the exercise and do it well.

11. Practice up and down the scale in your range.

12. When you understand the exercise, change to other vowels. You may find "ee" easier, or "oo."

Note: *The challenge is to fill up with air, concentrate on "spinning the tone," keeping the vowel pure, and the pitch "on target." The beginning tone is a rather light tone, adding the so-called chest voice as you get louder. Somehow the decrescendo seems harder; expect difficulty but keep repeating and you will appreciate your gradual success that empowers your voice.*

The breath pressure increases as one goes from soft to loud (pp to ff), low to high in volume; the breath pressure also increases as one goes from low to high in pitch. It takes time to train the vocalis muscle and your sensitivity to tonal differences. As you become more proficient you can add a five-note phrase. (Refer to Vennard.)

Use a five-note figure: C, D ,E, F, G or 1 ,2, 3, 4, 5, or do, re, mi, fah, sol.

The lower note will be soft, growing louder to the top note, then decreasing as one goes down the five notes until the beginning note ends the phrase softly.

You can acquire a voice that has strength, breath control, and flexibility as well as innuendo in both speaking and singing. You will discover in singing that you have improved your ability to sing even a scale.

Hum and Chew — Versions One and Two

Purposes of the Exercise

Version One: To release the voice and to prepare pitch, breathing, and tone focus prior to performance

Version Two: To assist the student or client who is having particular problems with pitch, breathing, and tone focus

A Brief History of the Exercise:

Version One is my adaptation of Version Two which was presented by Dr. Brodnitz at The Voice Symposium, Care of the Professional Voice, Denver, CO, June 1985. Version Two is a more detailed exercise which takes more time and repetition to acquire. This is directly from Dr. Brodnitz's demonstration. — **Dorothy Runk Mennen**

*Dr. Brodnitz was emphatic that the only way to change reflexes is through repetition. See Brodnitz, F.S.: Keep Your Voice Healthy. (New York, Harper and Brothers, 1953).

THE EXERCISE   CD: TRACK 7

The person can be seated or moving about as the exercise progresses. One should move freely. This exercise can even be done while moving down the hallway or off-stage.

Version One

1. Begin humming, then start chewing.

2. Continue, but add a familiar melody to the humming and chewing. Repeat the melody.

3. Continue humming and chewing a monologue or familiar passage. Be inventive. As you become familiar with the technique move about the room.

4. Before going on stage, hum and chew the words of the song from the play.

Note: *My experience has shown me that once this is learned it can be used in shortened form just before going on stage or entering a room.*

Version Two

1. Chew and make a monotonous hum: first with the mouth closed, then with the mouth open.

2. Continue humming and chewing. Count from 1-10 with the sound flowing out.

3. Hum and chew as if with a mouth full of food.

4. Hum and chew as if you are eating well-done meat.

Hum and Chew —
Versions One and Two

5. Continue the humming and chewing. Begin eating and talking at the same time.

6. Play an improvisation game of humming and chewing.

7. Read a paper or tell a story as if your mouth is full while continuing humming and chewing.

8. Repeat the story or reading with large, gross movements.

9. Be inventive.

10. Practice reading with feeling. Exaggerate the sense of melody. Use your hand to indicate change of pitch and inflection.

Note: *When familiar with these exercises, one finds that after a few minutes the throat relaxes, the saliva gland is functioning appropriately, the voice becomes more focused, and the pitch is optimal for that individual. The voice is "warmed up."*

Dr. Brodnitz's comments on pitch: "There is too much talk about pitch. Use the chewing technique. It finds the pitch."

His comments on breathing: "You get better mileage out of breathing if you think of chewing a long piece of spaghetti. How does it feel? (This may sound like nonsense but the image helps some people with breathing.) Try to think of shoveling air back in. Use your hands to visualize pushing the spaghetti into the mouth."

Improvisation from Primitive Sound

Purpose of the Exercise

To integrate breath, sound, and impulse

A Brief History of the Exercise:

This exercise was inspired by an exercise I learned from Carol Mendelsohn of the Roy Hart Theatre. — **Mandy Rees**

THE EXERCISE

1. With a partner, sit in two chairs so that you are face-to-face and about a foot apart. Decide who will be partner A and who will be partner B.

2. Take time to relax in your chairs, releasing your jaws, lengthening your necks, and finding comfortable alignment.

3. Look at your partner with an easy, soft gaze.

4. Partner A: Begin sighing a voiced sound through an open mouth.

5. Partner B: Receive the sound from partner A and answer back with an open-mouthed voiced sigh.

6. Continue exchanging sounds with your partner. Allow the sounds to change and develop as feelings and ideas emerge. Grunts, laughter, wails…all sounds are possible.

7. Feel free to touch your partner or get up out of your chair. Follow whatever impulses you have.

8. Now, when you are ready, bring this interaction to a natural conclusion.

Note: *The sounds produced should be deep, open, and primitive, without articulation. Students may attempt to use gibberish or vaguely disguised words (for example, making a "Wha" sound in order to communicate "What?"), but coach them away from this.*

Watch for tense jaws and tight lips. Coach students to make sound through an open mouth, rather than creating a closed-mouth hum. No effort to "refine" the sound need be made. The image of a caveman can help: an unsophisticated person with no language skills communicating a direct feeling from his/her gut.

Improvisation from Primitive Sound

Guide students to listen and react, to go with the moment without a plan. There is no need to be interesting or to entertain. Make sounds from the heart and the gut. Be affected by the other person. Focus on simple, direct communication.

This exercise reinforces many acting concepts in addition to serving as a tool to connect breath and sound with impulses. It certainly demonstrates how much power and information can be communicated through sound.

Vocal Mirrors

Purposes of the Exercise

To connect with breath

To connect sound to
    another's sound

To relate voice work directly
    to acting

A Brief History of the Exercise:

This exercise came about through a desire to find a bridge between the Meisner acting approach of really listening and working off the other, and pure voice work. Meisner used a verbal mirror exercise, so this is an extension of that into something more abstract and sound-based. — **Chuck Richie**

THE EXERCISE

1. Stand or sit back-to-back with your partner, although sitting is preferable because of closer contact with the back and spine. Take a few moments to get in touch with the other person's breath: feel its rhythm, length, size. Begin to let your breath become like their breath — don't push it, just let it happen. After you are breathing together, move on to the next part of the exercise.

2. Now, one person begins a sound, any sound, a vowel or a consonant, or a combination of the two, as long as it is not a word. Then the other person begins making that same sound along with them. The initiator will let that first sound lead to other sounds that can change shape, pitch, duration, and energy. Remember, just as in a body mirror exercise, it is the responsibility of the leader to make the changes in a way that lets the follower follow, and the responsibility of the follower to mirror those changes exactly. Begin now and continue for several minutes.

3. As you continue, allow the sound to move your bodies, but always let the sound be the primary force and let the body reflect that movement. You do not need to mirror each other's movement, although that may happen. Just allow the creation of shapes through the interaction of your bodies to accompany the sound. Let the sound eventually bring you standing, if you are not already.

4. Notice that as you go on, it becomes harder and harder to know who is leading and who is following. Let that happen, and let the exploration begin to change from a joint "soundalogue" to a shared, non-verbal dialogue. Gradually, let the movement take on the shape and relationship it might take on in a real dialogue or conversation.

5. Finally, find a need underneath the sounds and movements. Let these sounds turn into words. If you are working on a scene with this

Vocal Mirrors

person, let it be the words of the scene, or if not, just let it be an improvised conversation. Continue for several minutes.

6. All right, let go of the scene or the improvisation and go back to non-verbal sounds. Go back to creating shapes with your bodies and finally return to your original places, back-to-back. End with just your shared breath again.

7. Now, relax for a few minutes.

Post-Exercise Discussion:

What did you learn about your sound from this exercise?

What did you learn about your partner's sound and your interaction with it?

How did you do in the mirroring?

What happened when it became a verbal dialogue?

How would you apply this to your acting work?

Woo Woe

Purposes of the Exercise

To focus the breath

To energize lip articulators

To connect sound with
various body centers

To extend pitch range

To embody the sound.

A Brief History of the Exercise:

This exercise has evolved out of my combining work on various body centers (inspired by Linklater's "zoo woe shah" exercise and Frankie Armstrong and John Wright's "I love you / I hate you" exercise) with work on lip articulators (inspired by Lessac's "woo, woe, war" exercise). It has been modified and used successfully in undergraduate and graduate voice and text classes as a quick and lively warm-up which energizes the articulators and engages the voice. — **Karen Ryker**

THE EXERCISE

1. Stand with your body centered.

2. First, focus your breath from your abdomen to your lips by doing the following:

    a. Make a fist with your hand and place it against your lips.

    b. Blow through the fist with a short breath, as if quickly and efficiently blowing up a balloon.

    c. Repeat this several times, then drop your fist.

3. Now, think of sending sound from your abdomen to your lips by doing the following:

    a. Purse your lips while saying, "woo," "woe."

    b. Release sound while saying, "wow."

    c. Think of the sound as a ball that bounces off your lips with each "w."

    d. Repeat this several times.

4. Now, think of sending sound from different centers of your body. Send sound for each of the following, directing your hands and arms from the selected center outward:

    a. Send "woo" from your pelvis.

    b. Send "woe" from your abdomen.

Woo Woe

c. Send "war" from your chest.

d. Send "wow" from your face.

e. Send "why" from your head.

The "Ha"

Purposes of the Exercise

To center the body

To connect with breath

To extend pitch range

To focus attention on body, breath, space, and other students in the group

A Brief History of the Exercise:

The "Ha" part of the exercise (the end) was learned 30 years ago when I was working in Rep in England. Bill Zappa would use it when he led morning warm-ups. Additions and modifications were made during years of its use.

— **Annie Thompson**

THE EXERCISE

Regarding the "Ha" part of the exercise: At the end of the following sequence the group leader will wait with the group, sensing both breath and attention, gathering the group silently into a unit. When s/he senses that the moment is right, s/he will jump into a kabuki-like position (arms outstretched to the sides and legs apart in a deep plié -like stance). Simultaneously, s/he will release a vigorous "Ha" sound. The group's objective is to achieve this sound and movement simultaneously with their leader.

I find that explanation of the "Ha" is best done at the beginning of the exercise, although it can also be done in step 4.

1. Stand in a circle, hold hands, and close your eyes.

2. First, we will work on alignment, centering, and spacial awareness:

   a. Begin with consideration of the way in which the weight is distributed between and on the feet. Think of the weight of the bones of the skeleton descending through the feet and into the earth. Feel the anti-gravitational muscles of the body lifting the skeleton upwards. Take time to explore this tension, this balance.

   b. Gently rock back and forth on the feet. Stay balanced and aware, through your hands, of others in the circle. Circle your weight around the outer edges of the feet, gradually making your circle smaller. Think of a spiraling action moving upwards through your body and out through the top of your head.

   c. Return to stillness and be aware of your breath, low and steady. Drop the head forward and slowly let its weight tug on the spine and pull the torso forward until you are hanging upside down from the base of your spine. Now, sway a little.

   d. Take a full, deep breath and gently release it on a "shhhhh."

The "Ha"

Repeat this several times.

  e. Starting from your tailbone, and being sensitive to those on either side of you (you are still holding hands), roll up through the spine until you are upright. Try as much as possible to match rolling-up with those on either side of you.

3. Next, we will work on sharing breath and sound:

  a. While still holding hands and with your eyes still closed, imagine that the center of your circle is a pool of air from which you take (or inhale) and give back (or exhale) breath. Breathe.

  b. Gently begin to give a quiet "oo" [u] sound to this center. Be aware of how the sounds mix. Continue to do this with each new breath, being aware of the intermingling of sounds. Play with different vowels, different pitches, and different energies. Continue this step for as long as it is appropriate.

4. Let your next few sounds fade into silence. Stand still for a moment, feeling yourself in space and in relationship to those on either side of you. Release hands, but keep the contact going.

5. Now, we will do the "Ha."

  a. Slowly open your eyes but keep the focus soft.

  b. Wait for the "Ha."

  c. "Ha."

Note: *Laughter ensues and a sense of group presence usually results.*

The Wizard of Oz

Purposes of the Exercise

To explore the skull and nasal
resonators

To explore how "character"
affects the voice, and how
the voice affects a
"character"

A Brief History of the Exercise:

Kristin Linklater has outlined her approach to skull and nasal resonators in her book Freeing the Natural Voice, *and this exercise can be used as a compliment to that type of work. This particular exercise is derived from Carol Mendelsohn of the Roy Hart Theatre, who uses an "angel voice and witch voice" exercise to explore these areas. I have modified it, using the characters of Dorothy and the Wicked Witch of the West from the film* The Wizard of Oz. — ***Phil Timberlake***

THE EXERCISE   CD: TRACK 8

Dorothy

This is an exploration of skull resonators.

1. Vocalize, using an open vowel sound in falsetto voice, and imagine
   sending the sound out of the crown of your skull.

2. As you vocalize, place your hands on the top of your head and feel
   the subtle vibrations.

3. Now, imagine you are Dorothy from *The Wizard of Oz*. Vocalize in
   falsetto voice, using the text, "Run, Toto, run!" Imagine sending the
   sound out of the crown of your skull.

4. As you vocalize, place your hands on the top of your head and feel
   the subtle vibrations. Remember to stay connected with your breath.

The Wicked Witch of the West

This is an exploration of nasal resonators.

1. Vocalize, sustaining the consonant "n."

2. As you vocalize, place your hands on the mask area of your face —
   your nose, cheeks, lips, and forehead — and feel the vibrations.

3. Repeat using "m" and "ng."

4. Now, imagine you are the Wicked Witch of the West from *The Wizard
   of Oz*. First:

   a. Laugh, saying, "hee hee." As you vocalize, place your hands on
      your nose and feel the vibrations.

The Wizard of Oz

      b. Laugh, saying, "hey hey." As you vocalize, place your hands on your cheeks and forehead and feel the vibrations.

      c. Laugh, saying, "ha ha." As you vocalize, place your hands over your mouth and feel the vibrations.

5. Now, vocalize, using the text, "Surrender, Dorothy!"

6. As you vocalize, place your hands on the mask area of your face and feel the vibrations. Remember to stay connected with your breath.

Note: *At this point, endless possibilities for fun exploration exist. I often divide the class into two groups, facing each other. One group plays Dorothy, and the other the Wicked Witch, then the groups switch roles. The more physically involved the students get, the better.*

I also have each student play both characters, one right after the other, switching characters as quickly as possible.

If the class has access to a piano, the teacher can lead them up and down the keyboard. The different pitches often have an effect on the quality of the voice and the quality of the character being played.

Chapter 5

Articulating

Articulation of sound involves the tongue, lips, and teeth. In order for words to be understood they contain consonant sounds. If words didn't have consonants, we would speak in washes of vowels and diphthongs, and meaning would be very difficult to decipher. In order for clarity to exist in spoken language, we must form our consonant sounds with muscular strength, flexibility, and agility. Just as we exercise the muscles of our body in order to have physical strength, we must exercise our tongue and lips to have strong, clear articulation.

The following chapter presents exercises to help clarify and strengthen speech sounds. Richard Gang's "The Medial [t]" (5-1) addresses the single or double consonant "t" and how to arrive at "appropriate" muscle movement. Debra Hale-Thomas's "Tongue on the Wet Part of the Lower Lip" (5-2) stretches the tongue and opens the throat channel, while Betty Ann Leeseberg-Lange's lively "Consonant Conga" (5-3) allows for an energy-filled movement-oriented approach to a group consonant workout. Janet B. Rodgers's contribution of "The Joshua Steele Exercise" (5-4), which has been used by professional voice users since the 18th century, creates a rhythmic structure in which one can practice challenging consonant sounds and their application to words and phrases. Karen Ryker's "Quick Articulation Warm-Up" (5-5) is an excellent and effective energizer of the articulators, and Elizabeth Van Den Berg's "Moving Sound" (5-6) applies articulation work to the text while also incorporating improvised movement.

The Medial [t]

Purpose of the Exercise

To clarify speech by strengthening the pronunciation of the lightly aspirated "t" in between two vowels, as in the word, "better" and "butter"

A Brief History of the Exercise:

In as much as it is very difficult to teach the exact muscle movement for Skinner's lightly aspirated "t" between two vowels, I found a single way of combining sounds to arrive at the appropriate muscle movement. — **Richard Gang**

THE EXERCISE   CD: TRACK 9

American speakers in most regions substitute the [d] sound for the [t] sound, when the [t] is found between two vowels (such as "better", "butter", "...get a...," "...minute or...," etc.). However, for distinct or elegant speech, which is necessary for the speaking of classical material, period or style work, as well as certain dialects, the medial "t" has its own precise articulation. This [t] is found halfway between a fully aspirated [t] at the beginning of a word (and followed by a vowel) and the unaspirated [t] found before a consonant. The resulting sound is achieved by almost "flapping" the flat of the tip of the tongue against the hard gum ridge when producing the target sound.

1. To easily achieve the correct muscle movement for the medial "t," say the word, "get" and be sure to leave the flat of the tip of the tongue on the gum ridge. Now say the word "her" which, of course, begins with the semi-vowel "h." Simply allow the slight puff of air which results from the "h" to lift the tongue suddenly off the gum ridge.

2. Now, say the words rapidly in succession several times, and you will begin to experience the tongue slightly flapping against the gum ridge as you go through the [t] sound. If you are doing this correctly, you will feel a cushion of air exploding between the tongue tip and gum ridge at the moment you produce that final [t] in the word "get" before going through the word "her." This resulting tongue-flap is what you need for words like "butter," "better," "...what a ...," "...get a...," etc.

3. Now try saying, "Betty Batter bought a batch of better butter" and see if you can't keep the physical sensation of that light tongue-flap throughout the sentence.

Tongue on Wet Part of the Lower Lip

Purposes of the Exercise

To clarify speech

To free breath through the
channel of the throat

A Brief History of the Exercise:

I do not remember if I first did the exercise with Fran Bennett or Kristin Linklater ... if it came from another source originally or was created by either of them.
— **Debra Hale-Thomas**

THE EXERCISE   **CD: TRACK 10**

The body position is the same throughout the exercise. The exercise can be done while standing or sitting.

1. Select a sentence that is challenging because of the density of language or the complexity of articulation.

2. Say the sentence as you would normally, observing how the sounds feel in your mouth and the effort they require.

3. Now put the tongue on the wet part of the lower lip only, and speak the sentence as fully as possible.

4. Now, relax the tongue back into the mouth and speak the same sentence as you would normally, noticing the difference between this time and the first time you did it.

Note: *Because the tongue is being stretched, the airway is freed for more breath and as a result the articulators often work with greater ease.*

Consonant Conga

Purpose of the Exercise

To integrate articulation, breathing, pitch-range work, and physical, rhythmic movement

A Brief History of the Exercise:

I developed this exercise about 15 years ago and have been using it with students and professional companies ever since. It serves as an excellent, quick warm-up for rehearsal and/or performance. — **Betty Ann Leeseberg-Lange**

THE EXERCISE

This exercise is taught in stages to enable students to become comfortable with each portion before moving on to the next, and then integrating them.

The Articulation Portion

1. Begin by articulating consonants. First, the bilabial consonants (those made with the lips). Hum an elongated "mmm," then follow it with a staccato "buh," "puh." Again, "mmm," "buh," "puh." Repeat the three sounds in order until you begin to create a rhythm with them. Then, move your body to the rhythm.

2. Second, articulate the lingua-alveolar consonants (those made with the tongue tip against the upper gum ridge): "duh," "tuh," "luh," "nuh." Repeat these four sounds again and again, clearly, and with full facial resonance. Create a rhythm with the sounds, and move your body to the rhythm.

3. Third, articulate the velar-palatal consonants (those made with the back of the tongue against the back end of the hard palate). Hum an elongated "ngngng," then follow it with a staccato "guh," "kuh." Again, "ngngng," "guh," "kuh." Repeat the three sounds in order until you begin to create a rhythm with them. Then, move your body to the rhythm.

4. Next, integrate the three units, creating rhythms and moving your bodies as you articulate:

    a. Start articulating with your lips: "mmm," "buh," "puh." Repeat.

    b. Now, articulate with the tongue tip against the upper gum ridge: "duh," "tuh," "luh," "nuh." Repeat.

Consonant Conga

c. Next, articulate with the tongue against the back end of the hard palate: "ngngng," "guh," "kuh." Repeat. Find the rhythm for this group of sounds and then add it to the first two.

5. Feel the different places and resonances where you are making the consonant sounds. Repeat the sounds from the front of your mouth to the back while you create three different movement patterns with your body to the three different rhythms.

Integrating Breathing Work

1. As you continue to make the three different types of sounds, each with its own rhythm and movement pattern, observe your breathing patterns:

> Where in your body are you inhaling?
> Where in your body are you holding tension?
> How, and from where, are you exhaling?

Continue to make sounds and move. Adjust your breathing so that you are using as little physical tension as you can manage. Use only enough muscle tonus to create consonants, pitch resonance, and body movement.

2. Continue to make sounds and move. Observe your breathing patterns. Feel and hear when you need to breathe in order to keep the pitch resonance full, the consonants clear and crisp, and to keep your body moving in your rhythmic pattern.

Note: *This part of the exercise can be used for breath extension work, reduction of breath under tone, body and voice relaxation work, or breath placement work, as is the instructor's preference.*

Integrating Pitch Range Work

1. Continue to make sounds and move. Enjoy the sounds and the rhythms. Now, add a new sensation and play with pitches. Articulate your consonants and feel yourself experimenting with mid-range registers and pitches.

2. Next, slide up into your head voice, into falsetto, and enjoy the ping in your voice.

Consonant Conga

3. Now, slide down into your chest register and subvocalization, and enjoy the velvet in your voice.

4. Finally, return to mid-range registers and pitches, and feel yourself move back into your speaking voice range.

Integrating The Conga

1. Now that you have become familiar with consonant sounds, your breathing patterns and your pitch range, let's put it all together and do the Conga. Everybody get in a line, one behind the other, and hold onto the waist of the person in front of you. Step through the movement pattern slowly the first time and then speed up as you are able.

> **a.** On "mmm," step with your right foot.
>
> **b.** On "buh," "puh," step with your left foot.
>
> **c.** On "duh," "tuh," lift your right foot off the ground.
>
> **d.** On "luh," "nuh," put it back down.
>
> **e.** On "ngngng," lift your left foot off the ground.
>
> **f.** On "guh," "kuh," put it back down.

2. Now, do it again, repeating the steps until they become a dance — the Consonant Conga.

Note: *Repeat until all participants complete one full revolution of the space. To add variety, integrate the pitch range work while dancing the Conga.*

The Joshua Steele Exercise

Purposes of the Exercise

To practice using strong, clear articulation of consonant sounds within words

To master difficult words or phrases

A Brief History of the Exercise:

I learned this exercise while working toward my MFA in theatre at Brandeis U. The exercise was created by Joshua Steele, an 18th century prosodist and rhetorician.
— **Janet B. Rodgers**

THE EXERCISE   CD: TRACK 11

I. Select a consonant, word, or phrase that you find difficult to pronounce.

2. Practice the sound, word, or phrase using the following rhythmic pattern while employing strong consonant muscularity.

[repeat 4 times]	ᴜ	ᴜ	ᴜ	ᴜ
[twice x 3, then once]	OO	OO	OO	O
[thrice x 3 , then once]	OOO	OOO	OOO	O
[four times x 3. then once]	OOOO	OOOO	OOOO	O

Note: *The pattern should be read from left to right. The final utterance of each line is always a single beat.*

Quick Articulator Warm-Up

Purpose of the Exercise
To focus the breath and
energize articulators

A Brief History of the Exercise:
*This exercise was adapted from one presented by Meredith Monk in a workshop and
has proven to be a quick and effective energizer of the articulators.* — **Karen Ryker**

THE EXERCISE   CD: TRACK 12

I. Stand with your body centered.

2. Focus your breath from your abdomen to your lips by making a fist
with your hand and placing it against your lips.

3. Blow through the fist with a short breath, as if quickly and efficiently
blowing up a balloon.

4. Without vocalizing, move through the following series of sounds,
sending each sound through your lips, just as you sent the breath
through your fist.

      a. [p] [p] [p] [p]

      b. [f] [f] [f] [f]

      c. [s] [s] [s] [s]

      d. [t] [t] [t] [t]

      e. [k] [k] [k] [k]

      f. [ʃ] [ʃ] [ʃ] [ʃ]

Moving Sound

Purpose of the Exercise

To develop articulation for a particular piece of text

A Brief History of the Exercise:

This exercise is an adaptation of a singing exercise combined with some of Linklater's advanced work in Freeing Shakespeare's Voice. *It is designed for the beginning student's early work with any text.* — **Elizabeth Van Den Berg**

THE EXERCISE

This exercise is designed to develop articulation for a particular piece of text that a student is working on. It is introduced without telling the student that articulation is the goal of the exercise. The idea is to get the student to focus on the sounds and how they feel, rather than "just articulation." Implementing the exercise requires some improvisation and a solid understanding of consonant sounds on the part of the instructor.

Pre-Exercise Preparation

To prepare fro this exercise, the student will need a piece of text which they have memorized. They should "present" this text for the first time during the exercise.

1. One at a time, I would like for you to present your newly memorized text to me. Let's begin with you.

Choose the first student and allow them to speak their text. If the student is fairly unintelligible due to poor articulation, stand facing him/her and say and do the following:

2. Okay, we are going to go through that piece of text again together. Repeat after me, and mirror my movement.

All movements should be improvised based on the sounds of the consonants in the piece. For example, if the piece of text was from the Robert Frost poem, "Stopping by the Woods on a Snowy Evening," you could do something like the following for the first line, "Whose woods these are I think I know."

    a. *Instructor blows the "wh" while moving arms and body as if being blown by the wind. Continue "flying" while buzzing the "z" and moving while making the "w" sound.*

    b. *Articulate the "d" repetitively while jumping around the room.*

Moving Sound

    c. *"Fly" while buzzing the "z," quietly tiptoe on the "th" and, again, "fly" while buzzing the "z."*

    d. *Perform animal behavior with the "r."*

    e. *Quietly tiptoe with the "th."*

    f. *Sink to the floor on "n."*

    g. *Flop on the floor with "k."*

    h. *Squirm on the floor with "n."*

Face the student again, and, standing, say this:

3. Now, let's go through all the consonant sounds again, gliding them together very rapidly. I will make each sound first, then you repeat it back to me, quickly.

Do this two or three times, until the student can repeat the sounds back quickly and clearly. Correct any mispronunciation of sounds without referring to the consonant by name. Let the student think of them as random sounds, i.e., "wh," "z," "w," "d," etc. Begin slowly reintroducing the vowel sounds without informing the student that these are words.

4. Repeat after me: "wh," "ooo," "z," "w," "u," "d," "z."

Slowly build up speed until they recognize that the strange sounds they have been playing with are the words of the poem.

5. Now, let's speed up the sounds: "wh," "ooo," "z," "u," "d," "z." Do these sounds remind you of anything?

Note: *For homework, write down, articulate, and play with all the consonant sounds in your piece of text.*

Next time they present the text in class, it will be much easier to under-stand, yet not so "carefully articulated" that it sounds like a 2nd grade reading class.

Chapter 6

Exploring Pitch

Pitch change reflects intellectual and emotional involvement. Among certain segments of our population, it is not "cool" to express oneself with much pitch variety. Yet for the actor, professional voice user, and the singer, pitch is a valuable tool. Just as one to three pitch music would be very tedious, so is one to three pitch vocal expression. Strong, flexible articulation takes practice and so does pitch play. The exercises in this chapter give opportunities for you to practice expanding and developing your pitch range so that you will be able to express your full emotional range.

Pitch change within a vowel or diphthong of a word is called inflection. The first exercise of this chapter, "Inflection Exercise" (6-1) was discovered by Oren L. Brown in Richard Wood Cone's book, *The Speaking Voice*. This exercise encourages exploration of rising, descending, and steady pitch on vowels and diphthongs within words. Lissa Tyler Renaud's "Pitch Stretching" (6-2) encourages increasing pitch range within sentences. Janet B. Rodgers's "The Anaconda" (6-3), based on a Lucille Rubin scooping exercise, adds movement and scooping sound to explore a full voice-pitch. Her "Sirens" (6-4) takes the voice from its lowest to highest and back again while easing through the "breaks" or "cracks" in the voice. This exercise is excellent as a preparation for on stage screaming. The final exercise in this chapter, Jerold Scott's "Singing Exercise for Line Melody" (6-5) encourages you to sing your text with any melody you improvise or recall, thus liberating your spirit and breaking ingrained habits of pitch.

Inflection Exercise

Purposes of thes Exercise

To connect with breath

To extend pitch range

A Brief History of the Exercise:

This exercise was a basic one used by Richard Wood Cone, an elocution teacher, in his book, The Speaking Voice—Its Scientific Basis in Music, *1908, Evans Music Co., Boston, MA. It is of value to both the singers and speakers.*
— **Oren Brown**

THE EXERCISE   CD: TRACK 13

This exercise can be done while lying on one's back on the floor. In this position, the ribcage is naturally expanded.

1. With comfortably good body alignment, allow tidal air to expand the abdominal area, principally between the bottom of the ribs and the belt line. This kind of breathing supplies sufficient energy to initiate phonation.

2. Using one syllable words that start with unvoiced consonants, like "s̲ee," "f̲ive," "s̲how," etc., allow release of air to do the work. Do the following slowly in a sighing manner, using medium-firm intensity:

   a. Rising pitch   see . . . . ? lighter as it rises

   b. Descending pitch see . . . . ending firmly

   c. Steady pitch   see . . . . ! a straight-forward declamation

   Breathe between steps a, b, and c.

Pitch Stretching

Purpose of the Exercise

To achieve a heightened vocal sound by increasing the pitch range in a given intonation pattern

A Brief History of the Exercise:

Created by Lissa Tyler Renaud for her Voice Training Project — **Lissa Renaud Tyler**

THE EXERCISE   CD: TRACK 14

When we speak conversationally, we generally use a small to medium number of pitches at mid-range and mid-volume. When we speak excitedly, we use a broad range of pitches at the extremes of our range (high and low) and volume (loud and soft). Both drama and music serve to express heightened emotion, so it helps to practice shifting a sentence from a conversational to a heightened sound.

I. Say the following sentences conversationally and then, without the words, repeat the pitch pattern you've just used. Decide which pitch is the highest and which is the lowest.

   a. That's the stupidest thing I've ever heard.

   b. You said what???

   c. It's just not right.

   d. I've got a surprise for you.

   e. Can I help you?

   f. Go to your room.

   g. I lost my wallet.

   h. You shouldn't have to do that.

   i. Ah, that's the way.

   j. That's not very nice.

   k. You said you'd help.

Pitch Stretching

l. Don't even ask me to stay.

m. Look, Ma, no hands!

n. Can I have some?

2. Practice stretching the highest and lowest pitches farther and farther apart in this way:

   a. Speak the sentence all on one pitch.

   b. Repeat the sentence as you said it first, conversationally, with the highest and lowest pitches where you decided they were.

   c. Say the sentence with the high pitch one pitch higher and the low pitch one pitch lower.

   d. Repeat the last step twice more.

3. With the heels of your palms, try making slow circles in the joint where the jaw connects to the skull, with gentle pressure, while you are speaking. You may find that this will help you increase the pitch range you are using.

Note: *Over the next week or so, take note of the intonation patterns in ten sentences that you speak yourself and that you hear other people say. Make sure that you can reproduce them. Practice locating the highest and lowest pitches and then "stretching" them. See how the meaning of the sentences changes when you do this.*

The Anaconda

Purpose of the Exercise

To prepare the voice for extended vocal sounds

A Brief History of the Exercise:

This exercise is loosely based on a scooping exercise which I learned from Lucile Rubin (Professionally Speaking) I have added the movement and roller-coaster image. — **Janet B. Rodgers**

THE EXERCISE

This exercise should be done toward the end of a vocal warm-up.

1. Standing, allow the upper torso to drop down so that your hands touch the ground. Alternately twisting slightly to the right and left (as if you are climbing upward on a roller-coaster), move upward on the count of eight, with arms and hands making a scooping motion (hands side by side, palms down, fingers leading) with each count. Say "ha" at every count as you scoop up toward standing with hands and arms finally extended over your head. With each short scoop of, "ha" allow the hands to move with the scooping breath and sound. Take a small breath between each scoop:

   "Ha" (sip of breath), "ha" (sip of breath), "ha" (sip of breath), "ha" (sip of breath), "ha" (sip of breath), "ha" (sip of breath), "ha" (sip of breath), "ha" (big breath)...

   Now on one long, sustained "haaaaaa," allow the upper body and arms to twist and turn as if you are riding on a roller coaster from the top to the bottom of a twisting trestle. When you have completed the long extended "haaaaaa," let the upper body hang upside down.

2. Now rise up again on the sound of "hey," allowing one scooping movement with each breath. Use eight counts to move your torso toward standing with hands extended above your head:

   "Hey" (sip of breath), "hey" (sip of breath), "hey" (sip of breath), "hey" (sip of breath), "hey" (sip of breath), "hey" (sip of breath), "hey" (sip of breath), "hey" (big breath)...

   Now, on one long, sustained "heeeyyyyyy," allow the upper body and arms to twist and turn joyfully as the upper body hangs upside down once again.

3. Now, rise up again on the sound of "he," allowing one scooping

The Anaconda

movement with each breath. Use eight counts to move your torso toward standing with hands extended above your head.

> "He" (sip of breath), "he" (sip of breath), "he" (sip of breath), "he" (sip of breath), "he" (sip of breath), "he" (sip of breath), "he" (sip of breath), "he" (big breath)...

Now, on one long, sustained "heeeeeee," allow the upper body and arms to twist and turn as the upper body hangs upside down.

4. Now, rise up again on the sound of "ho," allowing one scooping movement with each breath. Use eight counts to move your torso toward standing with hands extended above your head.

> "Ho" (sip of breath), "ho" (sip of breath), "ho" (sip of breath), "ho" (sip of breath), "ho" (sip of breath), "ho" (sip of breath), "ho" (sip of breath) "ho" (big breath)...

Now, on one long, sustained "hoooooo," allow the upper body and arms to twist and turn as the upper body hangs upside down.

5. Now, rise up once again on the sound of "who," allowing one scooping movement with each breath. Again, use eight counts to move your torso toward standing with hands extended above your head.

> "Who" (sip of breath), "who" (sip of breath), "who" (sip of breath), "who" (sip of breath), "who" (sip of breath), "who" (sip of breath), "who" (sip of breath), "who" (big breath)...

Now, on one long, sustained "whooooooo," allow the upper body and arms to twist and turn as the upper body hangs upside down.

6. Slowly roll up to a standing position, using your abdominal muscles as your source of strength.

Note: *This is a wonderful exercise for energizing the body and voice.*

Sirens

Purpose of the Exercise

To explore and expand pitch

A Brief History of the Exercise:

I learned this exercise from Muriel Dolan while working toward my MFA at Brandeis University during the 1970s. — **Janet B. Rodgers**

THE EXERCISE   CD: TRACK 15

This exercise is best done while standing with feet parallel with the shoulders, knees soft and easy, the upper body centered, and ribcage alive.

1. Allow an easy breath to drop down into your breathing center. On the exhalation of breath, begin at your lowest pitch on an "m" sound. On this "m," go smoothly up your pitch range, easing through the breaks of your voice until you reach the highest comfortable sound in your pitch range. As you go over the top of your pitch, easily allow the jaw to drop, and open the sound into an "ah" as in the word "father." Maintain this open "ah" sound as you allow the voice to descend slowly through your pitch range, arriving back at your lowest pitch.

   The head should remain level through the ascending and descending pitch shifts. Keep the back of the neck released, soft, and easy throughout this exercise. If you run out of breath while going up and down your pitch range, simply allow another breath to drop in and continue from the pitch where you left off.

2. Take another breath. Then again on an "m" sound, start at your lowest comfortable pitch and allow the voice to climb through your pitch range. This time, when you go over the very top of your range, open onto an "ey" as in the word "hey." Descend easily through your pitch range until you reach the bottom of it.

3. Take another breath. Again, rise through your pitch range on an "m" and this time open onto an "ee" as in the word "me." After you reach the top of your pitch range, descend easily until you reach the bottom of your pitch range.

4. Take another breath, starting at your lowest pitch on "m," and slowly and easily ascend through your pitch range. This time as you go over the top of your pitch range, open onto the vowel "o" as in the word "mow." Descend in pitch, allowing a nice, easy exhalation of breath.

Sirens

5. Take another breath, allowing a nice easy release in the belly. Starting with an "m" on your lowest comfortable pitch, again slowly glide up through your pitch range from lowest to highest. As you go over the top of your pitch range, this time open into a "u" as in the word "who." Slowly descend in pitch, easing through the "breaks" in your voice.

Note: *It is important that you feel a sense of ease as you move through the pitches. If you have a big gap of no sound as you move from one register to another, just pull back with breath pressure and ease through the break. With practice, this shift from register to register will get easier and easier and there will also be less of a "break" in your sound. Also, with each successive practice, you might want to challenge yourself to increase (raise) your top pitch.*

Singing Exercise

Purpose of the Exercise

To increase line melody through pitch alteration, operative word stress, and variety

A Brief History of the Exercise:

I'm uncertain where the exercise originated, but I believe it's a Rodenburg/Berry exercise. — **Jerrold Scott**

THE EXERCISE

This exercise is excellent for readings which are coming across as flat and automatic. It is an advanced exercise (although very simple to do) in that I don't use it until after the student has had some basic exercise work in breathing, pitch, rate, melody, and resonance and the fundamentals are at a mastery level.

1. Stand and read the line(s) of text you're working with. Now sing, with a full voice, any melody that you invent or recall.

2. Now immediately speak the lines in a normal voice. Note the greater variety of expression the lines have.

Note: *Identify the causes of the change. Encourage the students to take more risks in line attack.*

Chapter 7

Projecting and Calling

We must first master the work and practice of the previous chapters before we can be effective at projecting and calling with the voice. In this chapter, you will lan exercises which will help you to project your voice while supporting the voice with your abdominal muscles in a controlled way while also maintaining a forward focus of tone.

Betsy Argo's "I Can't Hear You" (7-1) explores levels of projection while also pointing out the importance of final consonants and how to link them with words so that clear thoughts reach the receiver. Susan Stackhouse's "The Speaker Exercise" (7-2) asks us to create a megaphone-type speaker with our hands and then to explore an unfamiliar space while maintaining a forward focus of tone. Jennifer Thomas's "The Mommy Exercise" (7-3) encourages the forward focus of tone by exploring the word "Mommy."

I Can't Hear You

Purposes of the Exercise

To extend pitch range

To project and sustain sound

To clarify speech

A Brief History of the Exercise:

*This exercise is of my own invention, but the linking technique was inspired by Arthur Lessac. The exercise was originally devised to acquaint new students with three levels of projection: low, for intimate communication; medium, for small group communication; and high, for large group communication. — **Betsy Argo***

THE EXERCISE

Voice projection is achieved through an increase in volume, the raising of pitch, the focus of tone, and attention to the linking and sounding of all final consonants.

The operative sentence in this exercise is, "I can't hear you." By saying this sentence three times at three different levels, students learn what happens when a person raises his or her voice conversationally.

Depending on the age range and experience of participants, instructors may vary their use of terms and examples. If teaching a group, have the group spread out.

1. How many different voices do you have? Let's find out. I would like to hear three different levels of projection from you, from your low, intimate range, to a medium range, then to your highest level of projection.

Using the sentence, "I can't hear you!," I want each of you, individually, to repeat the sentence three times. First, to the person standing nearest you. Second, to a person across the room. And third, to a person outside this room. Let's take turns, starting over here.

Choose a student to begin, then go around the room until each student has had a chance to perform the exercise.

2. Did you consider what you did with your voice to change the three levels of communication? Your voice became louder, but it also became stronger, more powerful, and you covered more distance. You were able to increase the volume of your voice, acoustically, by taking and holding increasingly deeper breaths, supported by your diaphragm.

I Can't Hear You

3. What else did you notice in making your voice louder? Did you notice that you gradually raised the pitch as you increased the volume in projecting your voice at a greater distance? That's where we get the expression "Don't raise your voice to me" when we try to control an angry person in an argument.

4. Most of you, in saying the sentence "I can't hear you" to the person at the greatest distance from you, actually changed the message to, "I CAN hear you." You did this unknowingly, by dropping the "t" off "can't" because it was easier to project and seemed more natural when shouting (or projecting at your highest level).

   Here is where we learn how to sound all our final consonants by linking them to the word that follows. In this instance, what you will be saying is "I can't hear you." By using this technique of linking words, we can guarantee that the meanings of our sentences will be received correctly, without being misinterpreted or misunderstood, whether delivered at a low, medium, or high level of projection.

5. Now, we are going to repeat the exercise. This time, try to link the consonants at each level of projection.

   Repeat "I can't hear you" at the three levels of projection. Listen for the linking of consonants and coach as needed.

Note: *This is a great device for slowing down dangerously fast speakers who constantly need to repeat themselves in response to the question "What did you say?" or "Excuse me, I didn't catch that."*

The Speaker Exercise

Purposes of the Exercise

To project or extend sound

To explore an unfamiliar space and learn about its resonant qualities

A Brief History of the Exercise:

I have modified this exercise greatly from one I learned while a student taking the Advanced Diploma in Voice Studies at Central School of Speech and Drama in London, England. As Voice Coach for the Shaw Festival in Niagara-on-the-Lake, Ontario, I was very interested in exploring the resonant qualities of the three theaters of the Shaw (The Mainstage, The Courthouse and The Royal George) and so I introduced steps six through nine. — **Susan Stackhouse**

THE EXERCISE   CD: TRACK 16

This is a great warm-up exercise that can also be used specifically to explore forward placement of the sound or to identify the resonant quality of a physical space. While doing the exercise, ensure that the spine stays aligned, the shoulder, neck, throat and face are free of tension, and that the primary breathing muscles are used to support the sound. Keep a sparkle or smile in the eye throughout the exercise. You can take as little as two minutes with this exercise or as much as ten minutes. It is done in a standing position.

1. Using both hands, bring all fingertips together as if making a great big "O." Thumbs and fingers may overlap. From this moment on, this "O" is referred to as your "speaker."

2. Place this speaker up against the lower part of the face, with fingers underneath the nose, sides of the index fingers against the cheeks and the thumbs under the chin.

3. Stand facing a wall with toes approximately eight to twelve inches away. Without disturbing alignment of the spine and keeping knees unlocked, lean into the wall with your speaker intact.

4. Intoning with an open vowel sound (for example, "ah"), warm up the vocal folds and explore resonance as you get a sense of a vibration in your speaker. Play with a variety of notes.

5. Back away from the wall, keep the speaker intact, and hold onto the vibration sensation.

6. Begin to walk through the space and slowly allow the speaker to move from the face, mouth level, to a full arm's length extension. Always focus on the speaker and move the sound forward, along the roof of the mouth and out past the teeth and the lips.

The Speaker Exercise

7. At some point allow the fingers/hands to part; in a sense, creating "stereo speakers." Continue to explore the idea of keeping the sound forward and out, and yet filling the whole space. Swoop your speakers around in space. Play with pitch and the volume and power levels of the sound at this stage of the exercise.

8. Gradually allow the sound to fade to silence. Wait several seconds to enjoy and take in your surroundings. See everything as if for the first time. Hear the silence in the space.

9. Explore the spoken word. Find freedom of the text through the flexibility you now have with your voice.

The "Mommy" Exercise

Purpose of the Exercise

To learn how to project or extend sound

A Brief History of the Exercise:

I developed this exercise based on the teachings of Arthur Lessac.
— **Jennifer Thomas**

THE EXERCISE   CD: TRACK 17

1. Stand or sit, using easy, balanced alignment.

2. Hum on a medium-low, medium-intensity pitch with space in the mouth and gently pouting lips. The tongue should rest behind the lower teeth.

3. Let your jaw release easily as if its "strings" have been cut. Maintain the same medium-intensity pitch. The sound will change to "maaa." Keep the sound resonating just behind the upper teeth.

4. Let the jaw float back up and pout the lips again, maintaining the sound.

5. Part the lips slightly and gently press the tip of the tongue against the lower teeth while tensing the front of the tongue. Continue to sustain the medium-intensity pitch. The sound will change to "meee."

6. Cycle through the steps continuously, getting faster and faster. Begin to put meaning into the word so it transitions into speech. Release the sound strongly. Be sure to breathe when necessary.

Chapter 8

Integrating Voice, Breath, and Text

The exercises in the previous chapters have laid the foundation for skills that you will use in this chapter. The exercises in this chapter are designed to integrate all that you have learned and practiced. Now you will apply these skills to text work. Many of the exercises use Shakespeare as the example texts. Shakespeare's texts, like most classical texts, place tremendous demands on the actor for strong breath support, full resonance and articulation, and the appropriate projection of the voice. Indeed, these are elevated demands that require tremendous energy.

Kate Burke's "The Deal and the Truth" (8-1) helps the actor understand the premise of a sonnet and how to release the energy of thought (breath) into the text while leading up to the thought's conclusion. Tracy Donohue's "Dueling Choruses" (8-2) explores text using whole body and voice energy. Mavourneen Dwyer's "Painting the Text" (8-3) helps kindle spontaneous movement with words and the language of poetry, while Marian Hampton's "The Voice Outdoors" (8-4) encourages sensitizing oneself to an outdoor environment and allowing yourself to incorporate that awareness into vocalizing outdoors.

"Building a Wall" (8-5) and "The Glove Game" (8-6) were developed by Marlene Johnson as a means to explore Shakespeare's rhetorical ladders, operative structure, and "one-upping." Barry Kur's "The 'Stupid!' Exercise" (8-7) encourages keeping ends of phrases vital and alive while transitioning to the next phrase. Elizabeth Carlin Metz's "The Conduit" (8-8) integrates acting, voice and movement. Betty Moulton's "Breathing Out the End of the Thought Phrase" (8-9) encourages spontaneous free breath response to text. Mandy Rees's "Key Word Ball Toss" (8-10) uses volleyball-sized plastic balls to physicalize the text and give energy to it. "Listening/Breathing Transition to Text" (8-11), created by Ruth Rootberg, helps the actor connect with breath and then transition that breath connection into scene work. Natalie Stewart's "Lessac's Consonant Orchestra Scenes" (8-12) developed out of her desire to see students use language as verbal action. This exercise is based on the brilliant work of one of our foremost voice and speech trainers, Arthur Lessac.

Kate Udall's advanced exercise, "Act Every Word" (8-13), provides a useful way of connecting with the text by imagining its journey, while Lisa Wilson's "Core Belief Exercise" (8-14) helps us remove core beliefs that prevent us from fully expressing ourselves.

The Deal and the Truth

Purposes of the Exercise

To ground a Shakespeare sonnet in the here and now

To clearly identify the issue that the speaker is addressing, and to grasp the conclusion the speaker draws about the issue

A Brief History of the Exercise:

I created it, as far as I know. — **Kate Burke**

THE EXERCISE

The steps may be done during one long class period or spread out through two or three class periods.

1. Memorize an unfamiliar Shakespeare sonnet. Please avoid the more well-known sonnets.

2. Sitting in chairs in a circle, one by one, speak the premise or opening argument of your sonnet (Shakespeare's actual words), prefaced with the words "Look, here's the deal...."

3. Then, speak the final couplet of your sonnet, prefacing it with the words "This is the truth..."

4. Now stand up, in pairs, in front of the class. Speak the sonnets simultaneously.

Note: *The simultaneous speaking requires each individual to fight to communicate his/her sonnet, and the strategies chosen lead to interesting discussion, i.e., volume vs. articulation, esthetic distance vs. audience involvement, eye contact, interaction with the other speaker, physicality, etc. The exercise illustrates the idea that the text must be digested well to speak against, or through, another individual's voice.*

Dueling Choruses

Purposes of the Exercise

To learn to use your whole
  body to communicate
  words and images

To develop vocal energy

To explore text

A Brief History of the Exercise:

I got the idea for the exercise from Acting with Style *by John Harrop and Sabin R. Epstein. But it's not that exercise anymore. I guess I invented it to help the non-theatre majors in my Voice and Articulation class speak with more expression and energy. —* ***Tracy Donohue***

THE EXERCISE

This exercise helps the student slow down and 'see' each specific image in a poem or monologue. It helps the student fully understand the meaning of what they are saying. It's fun to do and is especially good with beginners — even high school students.

The following is a directive for the teacher.

1. Choose a poem or a monologue. Break the poem down into individual images/phrases. Write each image/phrase (using the words of the poem or monologue) on an index card. Number the index cards. Put the cards in order. (For example, using Hamlet's speech to the players, "Speak the Speech" goes on index card #1, "I pray you" goes on card #2, "as I pronounc'd it to to you" on card #3, "trippingly" on card #4, "on the tongue" on card #5 and so on.)

2. Split the group up into two teams. Have them stand in two lines facing each other. There should be at least 10 to 20 feet between the two lines.

3. Deal out the cards. If you have eight students, you'll deal out the cards as follows:

Team #1	Team #2
Student A - card #1, #9	Student E - card #2,#10
Student B - card #3, #11	Student F - card #4, #12
Student C - card #5, #13	Student G - card #6, #14
Student D - card #7, #15	Student H - card #8, #16

4. Remind the students to be aware of their order, based on the card number.

Dueling Choruses

The following are directives to the class:

1. You are dueling choruses like in a Greek drama.

    a. The person with #1 card, please step into the center facing the opposite team.

    b. Speak your phrase using your whole body and voice to communicate the meaning. Please use a gesture that can be repeated.

    c. Now turn and face your own team. Say the phrase and do the gesture again. This time the whole team will join in saying the phrase and doing the gesture.

    d. When you have finished expressing your phrase, please go back to your place on your team.

    Each student does steps 'a' thru 'd' with each of the phrases in the poem or monologue until it is finished.

2. Now exchange cards (Student "A" exchanges cards with Student "B" with Student "C" with Student "C," and so on) and do the whole exercise again.

3. Now that you have completed the exercise for the second time, sit in a circle so you keep the order of the cards as they were in the game. (Just have #1 close the circle with #2 and #7 close the circle with #8.) In this circle formation, say the poem/monologue again. Say just the one phrase on your card at a time. This time try to make the poem sound as if one voice is saying it. Please concentrate on picking up your cues and speaking with a consistent flow of vocal energy from person to person.

Painting the Text

Purposes of the Exercise
To connect body, breath, voice, and imagination with text

A Brief History of the Exercise:
I created this exercise to enkindle the spontaneity of being right there in the moment with the words of the text and in so doing, discover and cherish the sensuousness of the language of poetry. — **Mavourneen Dwyer**

THE EXERCISE

Each student is given a copy of Robert Herrick's "Delight in Disorder," which the group first reads aloud in unison.

> A sweet disorder in the dress
> Kindles in clothes a wantonness.
> A lawn about the shoulders thrown
> Into a fine distraction;
> An erring lace, which here and there
> Enthralls the crimson stomacher;
> A cuff neglectful, and thereby
> Ribbons to flow confusedly;
> A winning wave, deserving note,
> A careless shoestring, in whose tie
> I see a wild civility;
> Do more bewitch me than when art
> Is too precise in every part.
> — Robert Herrick (1591-1674)

1. Stand in a circle. In the center of the circle, I will place a tripod or an artist's easel (real or imaginary). Each person will take two sequential lines of the text (a couplet) following in order around the circle.

2. As your turn comes to say your lines, step forward into the center, pick up an imaginary artist's paintbrush and deliberately add to the portrait the item you are describing with your words. Speak slowly in a thoughtful, unhurried manner.

Note: *With an older group of students, I ask them to imagine either that a lover or a person they would like to make love to is standing in the center of the circle. Each person steps into the circle and actually unties, or removes a particular item of clothing from the imaginary lover, while they're speaking. No matter that the person being described in the poem is a woman. The student can transform the gender and the items of clothing in their*

Painting the Text

mind's eye.

If there are more students than couplets, I have them just start the poem again. I have found that this exercise never fails to bring the words of the poem to life. Automatically, the students arrive at something more lively, a variety of expression and spontaneity!

The Voice Outdoors

Purpose of the Exercise

To connect breath and inner impulse with text

To get away from manipulated voice and "canned" readings

A Brief History of the Exercise:

I developed this exercise in response to the problems of students needing to perform out-of-doors, but I have found it useful in connecting students with text and helping them to make the text their own. I first presented it at the ATHE Conference in Chicago, the year after I had presented a session entitled "The Voice Outdoors" at the ATHE Conference in San Diego, a session in which Bonnie Raphael and Jan Gist coached young actors from the Old Globe, using their own methods, in a beautiful outdoor Greek theater. — **Marian Hampton**

THE EXERCISE

1. Begin standing and start with a basic voice and movement warm-up, connecting with the breath, touching sound with the voice, using the various resonators, accessing the entire range of pitches, and concluding with some brief, well-supported diction exercises.

2. Choose two points several yards away from each other and run from the first point to the second, releasing a line of text (speaking it) as you run. Notice whether you feel tight in the throat or anywhere else in the body and make an effort to release the muscles in that area as you run back to the first place, again releasing a line of text.

3. Standing, with your eyes closed, notice the breeze playing about your face and release your entire text into that breeze.

4. Sitting on the ground, with your eyes closed, begin to notice the smells around you, and focus on just one aroma of all the various smells. Take that aroma into yourself, letting it become part of you and yourself become part of it. When you feel completely at one with the aroma, release your text into it.

5. Lying on your back, with your eyes open, focus on what you see above you — tree, sky, clouds, building. Take into yourself the vision of what you see and let it become part of you and yourself part of it. When you feel completely connected with what you are looking at, completely at one with your vision, release your text into what you see.

6. On your hands and knees, focus on what you feel beneath you. Sit back, with your eyes open, and find an object on the ground — a leaf, twig, blade of grass, or any other object. Explore the texture of that object, taking that texture into yourself and becoming one with it. When you feel completely connected with the texture of that object, release your text into it.

The Voice Outdoors

7. Standing, with your eyes closed, what do you hear? Focus on just one of the sounds that you hear. Begin to take that sound into yourself, letting it become part of you and yourself become part of it. When you feel completely at one with the sound, release your text into the sound.

8. Choose a place you'd like to be — in a tree, under a tree, on the grass, on a hill, on a step, behind a bush. Focus on that place, run to that place, and, as soon as you are there, release your text.

9. Choose any other place. Release text while walking to it.

10. Which sensory stimulus best connected you with the text and flow of images? Is it relatively easy or difficult for you to stay in the moment while releasing your text? As you compare the effects of focusing on different senses, which provide the most richness to your text?

Note: *Things to keep in mind about the foregoing exercises:*

1. These exercises may be done either by one person or an entire class. If done by a class, they should be done by one person at a time in steps 2, 8, and 9 above. Otherwise, these exercises may be done by everyone at the same time, with each student staying in her/his own space, not focusing on other students. These are meant to be personal explorations of text.

2. In a class situation, or in a one-on-one coaching session where there is a teacher, it is useful to discuss the questions following the exercises or any other questions which arise as a result of the exercises.

3. Any one of the exercises may be done alone or in combination with any other part. They may also be done indoors, although the results are most beneficial — and most observable — when they are done outdoors. The sensory stimuli exercises (steps 3-7) may especially be separated out from the others if there is not enough time to do all of the explorations.

Building a Wall

Purpose of the Exercise

To explore rhetorical ladders in a longer speech

To help identify operative words and key points in a speech

A Brief History of the Exercise:

I made this up while working with Oliver's speech in As You Like It. *Oliver is planning how he will bring about his brother's death in a wrestling match by hiring a wrestler to take him out. The speech is a list containing the many steps in his plan. Each step needs to grow out of the previous one and they all need to be tied together in a throughline of one big plan. Thus, he ultimately hopes to gain his objective, which is the removal of his brother. By embodying steps in a rhetorical ladder, this exercise helps keep the points in an argument specific, while also moving the argument toward a climax.* — **Marlene Johnson**

THE EXERCISE

1. Imagine that you are a bricklayer building a wall. You will start at one end of a room and build the wall across the length of the room. The wall will embody your entire speech.

2. Begin speaking your text as you mime placing a brick low to the floor. The brick gets placed simultaneously with each operative phrase or word in your speech.

3. With each new phrase/word, build the wall higher and higher. As you place the bricks, simultaneously move across the room as if you are building a wall across the room's length. You are now building and walking at the same time, illustrating that the points of the speech are building on each other. This embodies the tying together of all the separate builds or lists to have one great through-line of argument.

Note: *There is no attempt to mime "mortaring." It is the "placing" action, one brick on top of another, that is important, combined with walking as you "place bricks" or points.*

The Glove Game

Purpose of the Exercise

To clarify points in a long argument while moving towards a climax

To connect words to intention with a partner

To bring a sense of winning a game or one-upping (especially useful in flirtatious scenes, but could be used with any conflict)

A Brief History of the Exercise:

I made up this game up while working a scene between Orlando and Rosalind in As You Like It, where Rosalind is trying to cure Orlando of love. The scene is filled with bawdy references and is very flirtatious. But it is also filled with rhetorical lists — arguments in what Kristin Linklater calls a rhetorical ladder. It was useful in getting the actors to directly engage each other in a game that ripples with conflict and provided maximum opportunities to play off each other as the stakes got higher and higher. They have to build to a final climax or conclusion. — **Marlene Johnson**

THE EXERCISE

1. Sit facing each other with your feet on the floor and without crossing your legs or arms. Keep your jaws loose. Make eye contact with each other and breathe. Continue to do this as you play the game.

2. Imagine that both of you are wearing several pairs of tight gloves, one layered over the other. Imagine you have as many as 18 or 20 pair of gloves on. They are very tight on your hands and fingers.

3. First speaker, begin to say your lines while slowly starting to pull and peel these gloves off, finger by finger — first one hand, then the other. You may discover that various words become "operative" while removing each finger or every two or three fingers. There is no fast rule or outcome. Continue miming the peeling off, switching from hand to hand until your first set of lines is finished. As you finish, take the last set of gloves you've removed and either use them to slap the face or the lap of the person you are engaged with. (As one would do in the 18th century to provoke someone to a duel.) Make sure the slapping action occurs simultaneously with the final word. This keeps you from resorting to a falling inflection and allows the scene to build.

4. Second speaker, as soon as your partner has finished his/her lines and you have been "served" with the gloves, begin speaking your lines while peeling off your own set(s) of gloves. Remember to keep peeling gloves until you run out of lines. Then "serve" the gloves either into the face or the lap of your partner. This action is not meant to be violent and works really well to establish some playful sexual tension.

The "Stupid!" Exercise

Purposes of the Exercise

To increase awareness of
active, raised pitch
inflection at the ends of
phrases

To convert written text into
active spoken text

A Brief History of the Exercise:

I learned this exercise from a former teaching colleague, Marilyn McIntyre.
— **Barry Kur**

THE EXERCISE

I. Select a piece of written material.

2. Begin to read the selection aloud. Wherever you choose to pause for
phrasing, attach to the end of that phrase, "stupid!" Be aware of your
true grouping of words. This may not always be guided by punctuation.

3. Be sure to extend the energy of your delivery *through* the word "stupid!"

4. Take note of your pitch on the words prior to "stupid!" You will notice an
upward inflection of pitch, making the word prior to "stupid!" an operative word. Don't worry if this exercise leads to an inappropriate or even
angry interpretation at this stage.

5. Now read the selection again, without the insertion of the word "stupid!"
Keep the same energy (even if it's an angry one) in your delivery. Make a
deliberate effort to make the end of phrases more valued with inflection.
However, make statements. Do not make the inflections sound like
questions

6. Do the reading again with an interpretation appropriate to the speech.
However, do not interpret the reading in a journalistic, reporting
manner. Give all readings a sense of dialogue, as if you are talking to
someone with purpose beyond simply reporting.

The Conduit

Purpose of the Exercise

To integrate voice, acting, and movement with text

A Brief History of the Exercise:

"If you allow the words to breathe through your body, something magical may happen."
— Billie Whitelaw: Who He?

The following exercise was devised in response to the need to find instances where actors could fuse what they had been learning in voice, acting, and movement as an integrated experience with text. One of the difficulties I often encounter in training actors is the habitual censor actors frequently apply in expressing public emotion as a character. Actors often strangulate rather than release the emotion of a character. This exercise is designed to allow them to experience emotion via the text and breath as an integrated impulse. The breath is the foundation of this exercise. In essence, the body (breath, voice, gesture) becomes the conduit for the synchronized psycho/emotional impulse as expressed through dramatic text.

I have used variations of "The Conduit" at all levels from undergraduate to master classes. In graduate training, I tend to use it in the second year when students have more mastery over breath and placement and in releasing their bodies. There the application of the technique constitutes an entire unit, often in conjunction with verse monologues. In undergraduate training, I use a truncated version in beginning acting classes to convey the concept of integration, usually at the end of a week's unit on voice and Laban. I revisit it in advanced acting as preparation for working in Shakespeare. I have also used it with professional actors when in production as a voice director or director. — **Elizabeth Carlin Metz**

THE EXERCISE

To the actor-trainer: You will side-coach throughout this exercise. Be alert and supportive of emotional surges that may alarm beginners. Since emotional integration is largely the point, try not to permit dropping out. Once students have moved to their feet, it gets harder to side-coach the group, and you will have to circulate among them, side-coaching individually. It also tends to get loud.

To the actor working alone: Read through the exercise and actively engage the imaginative and visual aspects of the preparation, as well as the active core of the exercise. When you have learned the sequences, you will be able to take yourself through the process quite readily.

Pre-Exercise Preparation

I. Use a prepared monologue for this exercise, preferably something with high stakes. Shakespeare is especially productive.

The Conduit

2. Select the most dynamic moment of the text (one or two lines only) that strongly expresses the character's need or dilemma.

3. Fill in the statement: "I want _____." with the superobjective of the monologue, i.e., "I want to force her to forgive me." Now, distill that to "I want forgiveness." You will need to access that word and the lines on command.

4. Visualize the person to whom your monologue is delivered. Use someone whose expressions you know for your imaginary monologue partner, so that the implications of facial responses will be meaningful to you.

This can be an actual actor in the play, if it happens to be from a past performance, or whatever imaginary character you regularly play your monologues to. I do not do this exercise with text actors who are currently performing unless I am the director or the production voice director. It would be unprofessional to interfere with an established performance.

5. Lie down on the floor with your arms by your sides. Your spine should be as straight as possible. If needed, place a rolled-up towel underneath your skull or tailbone to correct for hyperextension in the natural curve of your spine.

6. With your eyes open, focus on the ceiling. Your eyes will remain lying down and focused on the ceiling throughout the exercise.

Grounding the Breath

1. While breathing, tighten, and release the muscles in your abdomen.

2. Now, tighten and release the muscles in your ribs.

3. Now, tighten and release the muscles in your buttocks.

4. Now, tighten and release the muscles in your lower back.

5. Now, tighten and release the muscles in your groin.

6. Imagine that your torso is an infinite cosmos in which protons and electrons are careening about and colliding.

7. Think of those protons and electrons as exploding energy, igniting desire.

The Conduit

8. Place one hand below your navel and gently jiggle the area. This is the seat of desire. Keep reminding yourself: "This is the seat of desire…This is the seat of desire."

The "seat of desire" is roughly between the pubic arch and the navel. The imagery you use for the seat of desire should be rich, but not sexual, as many of your desires will not be related to sex. When you feel you have released your tension and your breath is grounded, continue.

9. Now, with your free hand, trace the pathway of your breath by running your hand from the seat of desire up through the abdomen, then the chest, then the bronchi, then the trachea, then the chin, then out into space.

The Seat of Desire

1. Continue to keep one hand on the seat of desire and, with the other hand, trace the pathway of your breath as you visualize that you are coiled within your own torso. The space around you is dark, warm, and slightly damp, like the beach in a light summer fog at dusk. You should feel alert and ready, sensing space all around you.

2. Now, send your awareness to your back. Feel your back muscles expand into the space behind you as if you had wings reaching and stretching behind you.

3. Send your awareness in front of you and visualize looking deeply into the velvet light. Imagine a flash of the electrons and protons erupting like a meteor shower around you.

4. Send your awareness into your arms and reach into the atmosphere, caressing the light and the air. Now, send the light crackling and tumbling with the slash of your arms.

5. Sense the space all around you. See the flash and the whirl of the lights. Feel the electricity in the air and imagine the sensation of being coiled inside yourself, yearning to stretch and leap. Visualize the lights and collisions. Each collision is an explosion of desire — the desire to leap forth. At every collision, imagine that the words "I WANT" crackle in the air.

6. Let your breath fill the space around you, and allow your free hand to trace the pathway of your breath beginning in the seat of desire and ending extended outward, in the "infinity of space."

The Conduit

7. By now, your breath will be deeper and your exhalation longer. The physicality of your gesture has taken on more determination. Get in touch with the essential body inside you—the one that is coiled, alert, and yearning. Grab the root of the breath, match its strength with your hands, and reach for the lights in the distance.

8. When your arm tracing the pathway and your breath have power in them, continue.

Sounding: Intoning Desire

1. Continue to keep one hand on the seat of desire and, with the other hand, trace the pathway of your breath as you begin to visualize your monologue partner in the distance. S/he is walking towards you. Imagine your partner walking through the exploding lights until you can see his/her face clearly, as though it were in a close-up on a movie screen. Look deeply into your partner's expectant eyes. See the face become animated—the way the eyes look when your partner disapproves of you, and when they are forgiving; how the mouth looks when your partner is skeptical of you, and when it is loving. Visualize that moment just before your partner turns away in denial, and when s/he is about to come forward to embrace you.

2. Continue to keep one hand on the seat of desire and, with the other hand, trace the pathway of your breath. Remember the protons and electrons careening about in your body. Remember that every collision explodes in desire, need, and urgency. Now, think of the word that sums up your character's superobjective. With every breath, think "I want" on the inhalation and the word for your superobjective on the exhalation.

    a. Breath one: Inhale and think, "I want." Exhale and think of your word.

    b. Breath two is deeper: Inhale and think, "I want." Exhale and think of your word.

    c. Breath three is deeper and stronger still: This time, inhale and think, "I want," but on the exhalation, while thinking of your word, send a tone to your monologue partner.

    d. Now, take four or five rest breaths, after which we will begin this sequence again. A rest breath is a passive breath. Do not relax or break your concentration.

The Conduit

Repeat this sequence five times. Steps 'a' through 'd' should follow one another with only a few moments in between to give instruction during passive breaths. It is best not to let the students' bodies cool down or let their concentration drift.

Reaching for Desire

1. Now, we are going to repeat the last exercise, but this time, still lying down, follow through with your arms and your body.

   a. Breath one: Inhale and think, "I want." Exhale and think of your word. Follow through with your arms and your body, reaching for your partner.

   b. Breath two is deeper: Inhale and think, "I want." Exhale and think of your word. Follow through with your arms and your body, reaching for your partner.

   c. Breath three is deeper and stronger still: This time, inhale, thinking, "I want," but on the exhalation, while thinking of your word, send a tone to your monologue partner. Follow through with your arms and your body, reaching for your partner.

   d. Now, take four or five rest breaths and we will begin this sequence again.

Repeat this sequence five times. You may be following through with your arms and body so much that you begin to raise your upper body up off the floor. This is okay, but don't rise to your feet yet.

Speaking Desire

1. This time, we are going to repeat the exercise, but on the third exhalation, *say* your word for your superobjective.

   a. Breath one: Inhale and think, "I want." Exhale and think of your word. Follow through with your arms and your body.

   b. Breath two is deeper: Inhale and think, "I want." Exhale and think of your word. Follow through with your arms and your body.

The Conduit

c. Breath three is deeper and stronger still: Inhale, thinking, "I want," but on the exhalation, say your word to your monologue partner. Follow through with your arms and your body.

d. Now, take four or five rest breaths and we will begin this sequence again.

Repeat this sequence five times. Your physical follow-through and your vocalization of your superobjective should be quite strong by the fifth time through.

Desiring the Text

I. This time, we are going to repeat the exercise, but on the third exhalation, say "I want" and add your word for your superobjective.

a. Breath one: Inhale and think, "I want." Exhale and think of your word. Follow through with your arms and your body.

b. Breath two is deeper: Inhale and think, "I want." Exhale and think of your word. Follow through with your arms and your body.

c. Breath three is deeper and stronger still: This time, inhale, and on the exhalation say "I want (then your word)." Follow through with your arms and your body.

d. Now, take four or five rest breaths and we will begin this sequence again.

Repeat this sequence five times. Before the students reach the fifth time, say:

e. As you move to a standing position, imagine your monologue partner is on the wall in front of you, and carry the impulse of your exhalation through to your feet. Continue to gesture or move in any way you want once you are on your feet. Your movement may be realistic or unrealistic.

Desiring to Win

At this point, the instructor should walk around and make sure the students are using good vocal support and placement. When you see that each student is doing this and you tell them to move on, have them repeat the sequence again, but on the third exhalation, they should speak the one or two lines which em-

The Conduit

body the superobjective. Repeat the sequence three times. Begin a new sequence but on the third exhalation, the student should start at the beginning of his/her monologue and work through it like so:

1. This time, repeat the exercise.

    a. Breath one: Inhale and think, "I want." Exhale and think of your word. Follow through with your arms and your body.

    b. Breath two is deeper: Inhale and think, "I want." Exhale and think of your word. Follow through with your arms and your body.

    c. Breath three is deeper and stronger still: This time, inhale, and on the exhalation begin your prepared monologue. Follow through with your arms and your body.

2. Work to the end of a beat or full stop, then begin the sequence again, advancing the text into the next beat on the third exhalation.

3. Continue the sequence until you have reached the end of your monologue.

4. Begin the monologue again, this time without the breath sequence interruptions. Maintain the emotional and experiential throughline you have developed through this exercise.

5. When you have finished the monologue, lie quietly on the floor in a state of rest.

6. Begin a cool-down activity.

Note: *Instructors may need to help the actors visualize the collisions of desire — using whatever imagery enables them to connect to the physical idea of desire being ignited and directed into breath and then transformed into sound.*

Students should not push the sound off the throat, but should direct it forward through the mask and release it. Beware of vocal fry, glottal attacks, tense jaws, lack of intercostal support, clenched pectorals, and closed oral cavities.

Encourage timid students to raise the stakes so that they are sending the sound to their monologue partner on the ceiling.

The Conduit

Also, encourage them to make their physical gestures as intense as their need to reach their monologue partner.

If a student hesitates between the inhalation and exhalation, they may be resisting the exercise. Coach them to ensure that the exhale releases immediately on the crest of the inhale.

With students who have more sophisticated training, this exercise usually gets the breath rooted in the body, the body in the gesture connected to the breath impulse, and the emotional commitment centered in the body. It may well result in tears and expressions of emotional levels never quite reached before. Some students may find themselves shaken by the sensation of the emotion in their bodies — a sensation that is not usually cognitively remembered, but only physically recalled. This may frighten them. I take great pains to discuss the nature of emotion as a subcognitive experience that needs to be restored as a familiar sensation so that students may knowingly engage it. For this reason, I never do this exercise without text and character. I do not want students to be diverted into their own circumstantial histories by the evocation of emotional states. It is essential that as they begin to surrender to emotion there be a purpose. That purpose is relative to the basic desire of the character they are playing. The breath is the foundation of this exercise and is the bond that adheres thought, emotion, gesture, and language into one synergistic impulse rooted deeply in the center. The need is ignited with the impulse to breathe and the thought, need and gesture are embodied in the breath carried into speech.

Some students may get too nauseated to continue. Some may get too dizzy. Just deal with that as you would in any exercise. I usually have some chairs scattered around for quick sitting with heads between knees. Students will build up a tolerance for this exercise through practice.

Some students may want to bail out of this experience. I try to use my judgement. If possible, I side-coach the person supportively and encouragingly, assuring him/her that he/she has nothing to fear. If necessary, I do not force it. I would not expect this at the graduate or professional level, however.

Students with strong taboos about revealing emotion or surrendering to vulnerability may find this exploration difficult, but ultimately they will benefit immeasurably.

Repeated use of this exercise eventually develops the ability to release character and text quickly into integrated breathing and supported delivery. Students can readily take themselves and their text through the breathing sequences. My former students call it "conduiting the character."

Breathing Out the
End of the Thought Phrase

Purposes of the Exercise

To connect with the breath

To release the breathing
muscles

To allow spontaneous response
to text for free breath
response while exploring
text

A Brief History of the Exercise:

I cannot recall where I picked this up, or if I developed it from the influence of another exercise. I do know that I use "breathing out the end of the thought phrase" and have never heard it used by other voice teachers. We pick up suggestions like sponges and do not always know when and where we got expressions and exercises.
— **Betty Moulton**

THE EXERCISE

1. Speak each thought phrase of the text, in sequence, but (keeping the energy going) pause after each phrase to ponder what you just thought, or to form the connecting thoughts that might lead you to your next spoken phrase.

2. While you pause, let yourself breathe freely, at least two or three breaths in and out as you ponder or develop elaboration on the thought you have just spoken. Never hold your breath after you've spoken a phrase, even for a fraction of a second — I call this practice "breathing out the end of the thought phrase." All of your breathing muscles should be moveable at all times, never held rigidly or in suspension while you "prepare" for your next spoken line.

3. Then, when you have thought for a few breaths, speak the next phrase and keep "breathing out the end of it." Continue to think, think, think, and to keep your muscles moveable for breathing. New connections of thought can be discovered. Emotion has a chance to come from an intuitive response rather than a plan.

4. Then, when the thoughts and their connections are sped up, dispense with the extra breaths. The breath will now be freer to respond quickly and nimbly.

Note: *This exercise really shows the actor if s/he is unnecessarily holding the breathing muscles after each thought, however long or short the thoughts are. It is a good exercise for a class to do all at the same time or for one-on-one coaching.*

Key Word Ball Toss

Purpose of the Exercise

To energize a text

A Brief History of the Exercise:

Inspired by Cicely Berry's book, The Actor and the Text. — ***Mandy Rees***

THE EXERCISE

Pre-Exercise Preparation

Obtain three to six lightweight, volleyball-sized plastic balls, in a basket, for each group. Three balls per group is sufficient, though six per group is better.

Divide the students into groups of four, and assign each person in each group one of the following roles: thrower, receiver, ball passer, and ball retriever.

Throwers and receivers: Go to opposite ends of the room and face one another.

Ball passer: Grab your group's basket of balls and take it to where the thrower is. Stand next to him/her and get ready to pass balls to the thrower.

Ball retriever: Stand near the receiver and get ready to retrieve balls.

Throwers should use a simple piece of text for the exercise, such as Romeo's "He jests at scars that never felt a wound."

1. Ball passer: Give the thrower a ball.

2. Thrower: Begin saying your piece of text. Throw a ball across the room to the receiver on every key word in the text. (Key words are the operative words, usually the nouns and verbs in the sentence. In the example above, the thrower would throw the ball on the words "jests," "scars," and "wound.")

3. Ball passer: As soon as the ball is thrown, place another ball in the thrower's hands.

4. Receiver: Try to catch the balls. Then toss them to the retriever or the ball passer.

5. Retriever: Run after the balls that roll away and give them back to the ball passer. Balls fly around pretty quickly, so the retriever may get a good workout.

6. Thrower: Repeat your text four or five times, continuing to throw the

Key Word Ball Toss

balls on key words. Experiment with your delivery of the line.

7. Everyone rotates to a new position and the exercise is repeated.

Continue the exercise until each member of the group has been able to be the thrower and work on their text.

Note: *The ball is thrown while saying each key word, not just before or just after.*

Let the physical action of throwing the ball energize the voice and the intention behind the words.

The thrower should think about sending the ideas to the receiver, just as the balls are sent across the room.

Once the students have mastered the exercise, they can substitute full speeches or monologues for the single lines of text.

Listening/Breathing Transition to Text

Purposes of the Exercise

To connect with breath

To transition breath connection into scene work

A Brief History of the Exercise:

I created this exercise based on a need I perceived in my students. Every year the same questions arose: "What happens when I go onstage? Should I think about my breath? How do I use what I'm learning about my voice in acting class?" The "natural rhythm of breathing," as described in the exercise, comes from Linklater.

— ***Ruth Rootberg***

THE EXERCISE

This exercise is intended to serve as a bridge between the voice class and the acting class. It is a partner exercise that explores listening, giving/receiving, and breathing patterns. It is probably best done mid-way during the study of a scene.

When voice students, particularly beginners, become aware of breathing habits which have prevented spontaneous, impulsive, free vocal work, they sometimes go through a transition phase of focusing so much on their breath that their acting continues to lack spontaneity. There is some confusion about where to put one's attention: on the breath to improve the use of the voice, or on the scene partner, to find the truth in the moment. The fact is, when it comes to performance, you must put your focus on the other person. This exercise gives time to practice the scene using two styles of breathing. You will find out how each style can serve you to further your scene work.

Students who have used this exercise have found that while going through the first four steps, they sometimes feel disconnected from the richness of the scene. This will happen because the actor is not allowing the moment to influence the breath. Therefore, the breath will not fully influence the expressive quality of the voice. However, when they rehearse it a final time, both partners become very much alive and in the moment. Their voices open up, they feel centered, and their impulses fly.

For this exercise you will use two breathing "styles" which are described below:

Breathing Style #1 (based on the "Natural Rhythm of Breathing," a phrase/technique devised by Kristin Linklater) focuses on the breath itself, no matter what is going on in the scene. This is the kind of breathing you might find yourself doing at the beginning of a vocal warm-up. Relax and center yourself until you have found your Natural Rhythm of Breathing — the breath should release, and then there is a tiny pause. When the need for breath arises, yield to it. Once you have found this rhythm, there might be slight variations, but you stay with it to remain centered within yourself. Speak on the outgoing breath. Do not purposefully inhale or cut an outgoing breath short to

Listening/Breathing Transition to Text

speak. Instead, maintain your natural cycle. If you need to say more than you can in one breath, do not rush the incoming breath. Just keep going with your rhythm, eyes focused on your partner all the time. If you get caught up in the moment and leave your rhythm, find it again, and repeat the line.

Breathing Style #2 (breathing in what your partner gives you) allows your breath to remain alive to the impulses that arise from the scene work. Your active listening, need to communicate, and need to get what you want from your partner will "inspire" different rhythms of incoming and outgoing breath as you receive your partner's words. Pick up your cues according to the impact your partner has made on you. When your cue comes, immediately allow the need to communicate to take over. Do not wait for an outgoing breath to finish before allowing the new breath to come in. Instead, breathe in the need to speak, and then speak. Never hold your breath, waiting for your turn. Do not breathe in "early," anticipating your cue.

Pre-Exercise Preparation

Sit face-to-face with your scene partner. If your text is not memorized, you may have a table between you to hold the script.

Allow your eyes to remain focused on your partner, except when you need to read from your script.

You will go through your scene with your partner five times, alternating breathing styles twice, then applying the styles to the scene's final run through. In this way, you will each get to practice staying in your rhythm. You will also experience how to work actively, while your partner remains focused on his/her breath more than on you.

For the purposes of this exercise the word "line" means all of your text until it is your partner's turn to speak. It may be a word, a sentence fragment, a sentence, two sentences, or a long speech.

Part 1

1. First, partner A: Using Breathing Style #2, say your first line, fully active, using free breath. Partner B: Listen and receive while maintaining a "natural" breathing rhythm.

2. Next, partner B: Using Breathing Style #1, say your line when your breath cycle is available for outgoing breath. Partner A: Listen and receive with spontaneous use of breath.

3. Now, partner A: Using Breathing Style #2, say your next line, fully active, using free breath. Partner B: Listen and receive while

Listening/Breathing Transition to Text

maintaining a "natural" breathing rhythm.

4. Now, partner B: Using Breathing Style #1, say your next line when your breath cycle is available for outgoing breath. Partner A: Listen and receive with spontaneous use of breath.

5. Continue in this fashion until the end of the scene.

Part 2

1. Remain seated and get ready to begin the scene again.

2. This time, each of you should use active listening and free, responsive breathing.

3. Begin the scene when you are ready.

   This will allow you to find the rhythm of the scene again before moving on to Part 3.

Part 3

Part 3 is the same as part 1, but now you are going to reverse roles.

1. First, partner B: Using Breathing Style #2, say your first line, fully active, using free breath. Partner A: Listen and receive while maintaining a "natural" breathing rhythm.

2. Next, partner A: Using Breathing Style #1, say your line when your breath cycle is available for outgoing breath. Partner B: Listen and receive with spontaneous use of breath.

3. Now, partner B: Using Breathing Style #2, say your next line, fully active, using free breath. Partner A: Listen and receive while maintaining a "natural" breathing rhythm.

4. Now, partner A: Using Breathing Style #1, say your next line when your breath cycle is available for outgoing breath. Partner B: Listen and receive with spontaneous use of breath.

Part 4

Part 4 is the same as part 2.

1. Remain seated and get ready to begin the scene again.

2. This time, each of you should use active listening and free,

Listening/Breathing Transition to Text

responsive breathing.

3. Begin the scene when you are ready.

*This will allow you to find the rhythm of the scene again before |
moving on to Part 5.*

Part 5

1. Stand up.

2. Partner A and partner B: Using Breathing Style #2, put the scene up
on its feet with blocking, props, etc.

3. Begin the scene when you are ready and play it fully.

Variation 1

To shorten the exercise to only three run-throughs, you can cut out
Parts 2 and 4. This will give each of you a turn of staying in your own
rhythm, then putting the scene on its feet.

Variation 2

To shorten the exercise to only two run-throughs, you can run the
scene once with both of you staying in your own rhythm at the same
time, then putting the scene on its feet.

FOLLOW-UP

Sit down with your partner and discuss your experiences:

What happened when you stayed in your own rhythm?

What was it like to play actively but have your partner stay in
his/her own rhythm?

Did the scene play differently on its feet at the end than during previous rehearsals? How?

What did each of you notice about the use of your voice?

Were there any significant changes in rehearsal/class presentation of
this scene following the exercise?

Notice the changes in your approach to breathing through new
scenes.

Lessac's Consonant Orchestra Scenes

Purpose of the Exercise

To clarify speech and to connect Lessac's Consonant Orchestra exercise into acting on the word

A Brief History of the Exercise:

This exercise was inspired based on wanting to show actors the direct application of Lessac's Consonant Orchestra. It came from a desire to see them use the language for their actions. It was also inspired by the Patrick Tucker Shakespeare work where the actors only learn their lines and cues, and don't know or can't anticipate what is coming next. — **Natalie Stewart**

THE EXERCISE

A list of scenes appears at the end of this exercise.

Pre-Exercise Preparation

Before beginning this exercise, students should familiarize themselves with Lessac's Consonant Orchestra exercise. This can be found in his book, The Use and Training of the Human Voice, *pages 63-121.*

Discuss playing consonant sounds in order to affect someone. For example, play the [n] sound in "town" to calm someone, play the [kt] sound in "tact" to intimidate someone.

Discuss acting "on" the word, using the sounds of the word to play the action.

Copy each of the scenes (found after these instructions) and cut each scene down the middle.

Divide your students into pairs, giving the students in each pair their half of the scene, their character designation (partner A or B), and the situation for the scene ("A is trying to 'pick-up' B.")

1. Do not show your partner your copy of the script.

2. Separate from your partner, spreading out to find your own space.

3. Begin scoring the words on your script, underlining playable consonants.

4. Next, based on the situation for your scene, practice playing your consonant sounds with various tactics — to warn, to seduce, to belittle, etc.

5. Find your partner and without showing them your copy of the script, discuss a setting for the scene and set that up, if possible. Do not decide what will happen in the scene; each actor should listen and respond to the other without pre-planned actions or reactions.

Lessac's Consonant Orchestra Scenes

6. When it is your turn to go, set up your space, tell the rest of the class what your setting is, and begin the scene.

7. Partner A will begin with the first word on his/her list, then partner B will respond with the first word on his/her list. Partner A continues with the next word, and so on, continuing back and forth until the end of the scene.

Scene #1

(*Possible situation: A is trying to "pick-up" B.*)

A	B
Yum	None
Moon	Doom
Love	Leave
Undress	Insane
Lust	Last
Live	Please
Seize	Grand
Loves	Beans
Hands	Compliment
Envision	Alone
Understand	Can't
Unison	Undone
Wonderful	Crafty
Sinful	Laugh
Loves	Yum

Scene #2

(*Possible situation: A thinks B has just stolen something from him/her.*)

A	B
Gone	And
Find	Understand
Give	Aghast
Please	Insane
Ghosts	Guess
Laugh	Painful
Pretend	Cares
Believe	Sincere
Fanciful	Enough
Phantom	Ends
Lines	Nonsense
Give	Ruined
Demand	Thief
None	Crazed
Invisible	Detest
Fine	Gone

Lessac's Consonant Orchestra Scenes

Scene #3

(*Possible situation: A has just cut B's hair.*)

A	B
Done	Grand
Feast	Ghastly
Insane	Mountain
Incredible	Madman
Leave	Vampire
Insulted	Deserves
Give	Can't
Thief	Gloved-hand
Talented	Laugh
Fists	Stop
Gloves	Again
Off	Yes
Boss	Relief
Dumb	Pardon
Buzz	Improvement
Done	Grand

Scene #4

(*Possible situation: A has been waiting for B, who is late. A suspects B of something.*)

A	B
Time	Eleven-fifteen
Was	Please
Explain	Individual
Insipid	Decisions
Unison	Alone
Whose	Those
Sleaze	Amazed
Sinful	Accused
Abused	Unbelievable
Explanation	None
Leave	Love
Bum	Unjust
Condemn	Understand
Insane	Sympathize
Impossible	End
Crafty	Leave
Pause	Resolved
Unresolved	

Lessac's Consonant Orchestra Scenes

Scene #5

(*Possible situation: B is auditioning for A.*)

A	B
Name	Sssss
Pardon	Sam
Begin	Nervous
Understand	Important
Brilliant	Unnerved
Please	Friends Romans
Stop	Lend
Indicating	Was
Objective	Understand
Again	Friends Romans
Ghastly	Yes
Unbearable	Indicating
Contrived	Again
Fine	Friends Romans
Rotten	Chance
Can't	Explain
Maim	Actress
Indeed	Talented
Laugh	Beast
Perceptive	Gone
Fun	

Act Every Word

Purpose of the Exercise

To connect with imaging the text

A Brief History of the Exercise:

I learned this exercise from Joanna Weir. It is a very useful way of connecting with text. It forces one to be very specific and precisely image the journey of the text. With beginners, I use it with haiku; with advanced students, I use it with any piece of text.

— ***Kate Udall***

THE EXERCISE

The exercise is simple. Students must physically act out every word of the text. Usually, I tell them to omit the "small" words, although they can be quite useful, too. I tell students to envision that they are performing bad theatre for very young children. The personification of the word must be in the whole body, not just the arms or the face. It can be literal (for the word "clock" they can turn their body into a clock face) or imaginative (a full body impulse that comes from feeding the word "clock" into themselves).

I. Begin delivering a prepared piece of text, acting out every word. Embody each word very specifically, speaking as you move.

2. Begin the text again, but this time, go a little faster, moving from one word to the next without losing the clarity and specificity of each individual word.

3. Now, begin the text again, but this time, stand and speak the text without moving. Challenge yourself to keep the clarity of the journey through the words.

Core Belief Exercise

Purpose of the Exercise

To help connect the free emotional life of voice and movement to the text

A Brief History of the Exercise:

This exercise was inspired by Joy Gardner at the VASTA workshop in 1998. Joy worked with the healing of old wounds by having you state the psychological core belief that inhibits your growth in the world. For example, if your inhibitive core belief is 'only really attractive people deserve to find love,' you can replace that with 'I am beautiful inside and deserve love.' — **Lisa Wilson**

THE EXERCISE

Pre-Exercise Preparation

This exercise works best mid-way through the rehearsal process, as the exercise ends with the actors taking what they've learned into the "confines" of the stage setting.

Actors should find a partner to work with for this exercise and a scene from the play they are rehearsing together. Each actor will need their own copy of the scene, and a pen/pencil.

1. Separate from your partner, and take a few minutes to analyze your character's lines in the scene. Circle the lines that provide a key to your character's core beliefs about the world and his/her place in it.

2. Using those lines, develop one statement that embodies the character's core belief.

Using Hamlet, *here are a few examples. One might choose the following lines on which to base the core belief:*

"The time is out of joint–O cursed spite
That ever I was born to set it right!"
    Shakespeare, Hamlet, *II.i.*

Core belief statement: I am the victim of fortune and have no choice but to revenge my father's death.

"Oh, what a rogue and peasant slave am I!
....for it can not be
But I am pigeon-liver'd, and lack gall
To make Oppression bitter, or ere this
I should 'a fatted all the region kites
With this slaves offal."
    Shakespeare, Hamlet, *II.ii.*

Core Belief Exercise

Core belief statement: I am a coward if I do not avenge my father's murder and my mother's dishonor.

3. Now, find your partner again and, in character, using your own words, state your core belief to his/her character. Do this within the context of the scene relationship and allow it to move into a physicalized interaction (i.e., begging, oppressing, holding the other actor).

4. Repeat the statement and the action, letting it grow until the core belief takes root and can be heard in your vocal release.

5. Now, still speaking and physicalizing your core belief statement, move into pure, open vocal expression, using open vowel sounds.

6. Now, it's the other actor's turn. In character, state your core belief to the other character. Do this within the context of the scene relationship and allow it to move into a physicalized interaction.

7. Repeat the statement and the action, letting it grow until the core belief takes root and can heard it in your vocal release.

8. Now, still speaking and physicalizing your core belief statement, move into pure, open vocal expression, using open vowel sounds.

9. Now, using the words of the author, begin the scene, both of you playing strongly from the core belief point-of-view.

   It may be useful to identify and play with repeated vowel sounds from the text. Suggest an open vowel sound if the actor is closing off the voice rather than opening as s/he experiences stronger physicalization.

   As the actors repeat the scene, continue to help them release their voice, breath, physical and emotional connection through the text. Step in and suggest physical action when the actors seem to need guidance, and give them open sounds to work with. Take the scene between Hamlet and the Ghost in I.iv., for example. It would be useful to explore the Ghost challenging Hamlet, and the subsequent subjugation of Hamlet; the torment of Hamlet by the Ghost could be physicalized in a way which might not be appropriate to "realistic" staging.

10. Now, let's repeat the scene again, within the "confines" of the staging. Try to allow more of the vocal life and physicalization of the core belief to live in the scene.

Core Belief Exercise

FOLLOW-UP

Post-exercise Discussion

How was physicalization linked to the text?

Did the words feel more visceral?

Did your breath come from a more emotional place?

What type of movement seemed to aid the clarity of the scene?

How can you carry that over into the real stage movement for this scene?

Chapter 9

Integrating Voice and Movement

All of the exercises in this chapter involve gestural movement or locomotion. One of my favorite exercises, Frankie Armstrong's "Gossip Hoeing" (9-1), creates a "playful, non-threatening, non-judgmental opportunity" for students to extend their vocal range while creating a sense of community. Marian Hampton's "Voice Leading the Body" (9-2) can be used in early voice training; the exercise connects voice and body with sound and lets the sound suggest movement. Jim Johnson's "Connections" (9-3) integrates mind, body, voice, and text by asking the participants to physicalize each word of the text, literally, abstractly, and bizarrely. Joan Melton's "Jog and Sound" (9-4) asks the participants to jog while discovering abstract sounds to accompany the movement. Christine Morris's "Elephant Walking Chant" (9-5) is based on an old chant used in India by elephant-keepers moving their elephants from one place to another. Floortje Nyssen's playful "Chewing Gum Bubble" (9-6) stimulates the imagination while freeing the voice to make sounds. Karen Ryker's "Across the Floor" (9-7) explores many ways of vocalizing locomotion from one place to another, and Lisa Wilson's "Emotional Flow" (9-8) helps to release the tensions that restrict the release of emotion.

Gossip Hoeing

Purposes of the Exercise

To create a playful, non-threatening, non-judgmental opportunity for students/participants to extend vocal range and color

To help students discover that chatting, gossiping, hollering, chanting, and singing are all on a continuum

To recreate a sense of community and continuity

A Brief History of the Exercise:

I used the simple potent call and response from the very outset of my workshops in 1975. This was based on the warm-up exercises learned from Ethel Raim's Balkan Singing Workshops. For the first two years of workshops, I had a room with chairs and we moved between sitting and standing. I then moved to a dance studio with no seating. It got tiring either standing or sitting on the floor for the entire duration so I started to use simulated work movements. Initially, the calls were "hay" or "ee," but over the years they have elaborated into made-up language with a much wider range of sounds, colors, and expression. — **Frankie Armstrong**

THE EXERCISE

This would most likely be within the first hour or so following a playful-style body/voice warm-up. This would have ended with "copy cat" sounds which create the call-and-response pattern.

1. Now I'd like us to come into a circle and imagine that we are people of a pre-industrial village community or somewhere in the world where people still work together in the fields. Today we need to turn the top soil, so imagine you have a hoe or rake — the soil is lovely and soft, so it isn't hard work. You can keep arms and shoulders relaxed as you sway in and out. Have strong but flexible legs and really sense the earth under your feet and make sure that your knees are soft. I'll continue calling for you to respond to — we'll simply have the additional rhythm and sway as we work. Now, at this point, I want to say that if anyone here has been told they're 'tone deaf,' can't hold a tune, or simply aren't confident of holding a melody, this doesn't matter at all. I shall call, gossip, holler, yodel, chant and who knows what else. You simply send it back with the intended or unintended harmonies.

2. I'll say "forward and back" a few times so we can coordinate our work action, then you echo my calls.

3. This is where it becomes difficult in the print version to convey the sounds that I use. I've written some phrases below as an example. Imagine how they're being spoken, chanted, or sung. Some move between these tones in the course of one call. I gradually increase the range both pitch and color/timbre-wise and continue to segue between the heightened spoken and sung voice.

   e.g., Hay za shama. Repeat.
   Sha day maanow. Repeat.
   Seska me leshco. Repeat.
   Na taylo horska. Repeat.

Gossip Hoeing

Notes: *I make these sounds up on the spur of the moment and continue this process for some four to five minutes so the sounds can gather impetus and energy.*

The thing that still excites me about this exercise, which has become the "leitmotif" of my work, is the number of people over the years who, despite being convinced they're "tone deaf," have within an hour or so of the start of a workshop found themselves following quite complicated pitches perfectly. This was summed up beautifully by a woman who said: "I came here convinced I couldn't sing — and you snuck it up on me — and I can!" She was right.

Voice Leading the Body

Purpose of the Exercise

To connect voice and body with sound

A Brief History of the Exercise:

I use this exercise early in voice training as a way of connecting the voice with the body and letting the voice suggest movement to the body rather than vice versa, as we usually do. It began with a series of sound exercises in Kristin Linklater's text, Freeing the Natural Voice, *to which I added the idea of developing movement suggested by the voice sounds and motivated only by the voice sounds.*

— *Marian Hampton*

THE EXERCISE

1. Sitting comfortably on the floor, begin making as many different sounds with your articulators as possible, using tongue, teeth, lips, mouth, nasal cavities and pharynx to produce unvoiced (just on the breath) sounds. Continue exploring these sounds for a while.

2. Begin to add an "ee" vowel into the mix.

3. After a while, add an "ay" vowel as well.

4. Then add an "oh" vowel.

5. Then begin to develop several favorite sound combinations (three or four) and let each sound combination suggest its own particular movement/s. Let the sound lead the movement. Be sure you make no movements except what the sounds themselves cause you to make.

6. We're still sitting and moving on the floor, but now you may begin to let the movements gradually bring you up to a standing position.

7. Then, you may begin to let the sounds move you about the floor. Be sure not to walk or make any movements with the arms, hands or head which are not initiated by the sounds you are using.

8. Finally, you may begin to take these sound and movement combinations into a piece of acting text, keeping the focus on the sounds and movements they cause. Let go of clarity of diction for the moment, so that the sounds and movement gradually become the text.

Note: *In a class situation, it's useful at this point to ask the students to stay in their own process, and share a piece of their text, one by one. The sound and movement combinations should dominate and inform the text. I go around the room and tap each person gently on the shoulder to begin, after the previous person has shared her/his text. It's often useful to discuss afterward what discoveries the student/s may have made during this exercise.*

Connections

Purpose of the Exercise
To connect mind, breath, body and voice with text

A Brief History of the Exercise:
I kind of built this myself, but it's obviously closely linked to 'Sound and Movement,' 'Dropping In,' and 'My House is Burning.' — **Jim Johnson**

THE EXERCISE

1. Go through each word in a sentence or line of text physicalizing a very literal meaning of each word. Repeat each word until you find something physical which connects you to the word.

2. Now go through the same line and physicalize an abstraction of each word. Repeat the word until you have become clear with the physical expression.

3. Repeat the physicalization of each word again, but this time let it twist into some other bizarre meaning that is not in the text at all. This may entail seeking alternate meanings for the word, morphing it into another word that sounds similar, or even breaking up the sounds of the words and exploring them individually.

4. Go through the entire text, word by word, and attach at least two distinctly different experiences of expression or content to each word using any of the three methods with which you have already experimented.

5. Once you have completed a chunk of the text, go through the entire chunk aloud, repeating each word until one of these "connections" is revisited.

6. Repeat the same text, elongating each word until you find the connection.

7. Repeat the text again, perhaps only finding a few of the connections.

Note: *Usually by step #7, the students have a greater connection to the text and can more easily experience the text as they say it. Sometimes this slows them down considerably and eliminates "rushing."*

Jog and Sound

Purposes of the Exercise

To energize the body

To get breath flowing

To wake up the pitch range

To find an easy, noiseless
   inhalation

A Brief History of the Exercise:

This exercise is adapted from an exercise by Angela Downey in her London Workshop for Advanced Diploma in Voice candidates, 1990. — **Joan Melton**

THE EXERCISE   CD: TRACK 18

1. Jog around the room, arms and legs loose. Move arms about, overhead, sideways, etc.

2. Blow breath out with each jog.

3. Then change breath to sound. Play through range, one sound per jog and one breath per jog. This will be very rhythmic.

Elephant Walking Chant

Purposes of the Exercise

To show how movement can become an extension of sound

A Brief History of the Exercise:

I learned this exercise from Venice Manley, singer and teacher extraordinaire, who is based in London. She said that it was an old chant used in India by elephant-keepers moving their elephants from one place to another. — **Christine Morris**

THE EXERCISE

The music for the Elephant Walking Chant appears at the end of the exercise.

I often use this as a group exercise, especially when working with people who believe they cannot sing. I introduce it by simply beginning to sing it, and I find that people quickly begin to join in as they feel ready. It is simple and repetitive, making it easy to join in, yet it is challenging and engaging. The timing is not always what one might expect and there is a tricky little E-flat in the third measure, which becomes a D in the fourth. As it is a walking chant, movement simply becomes an extension of the sound, and eventually I find that everyone can be singing and walking together easily. This can go on for a long and pleasurable time, with "non-singers" participating in a full, relaxed way. It is only at the end that I tell them what the chant is called, and by that time, the reaction is often, "Of course!"

1. Spread out within the space, so that you are not too close to other people.

2. Listen to what I sing, then begin singing when you want to join in.

3. When you feel ready, begin walking around in the space to the rhythm of the chant.

4. Feel free to improvise vocally and physically, seeing where the activity takes you.

5. Continue chanting and walking until the chant dies out.

Elephant Walking Chant

[bi   wa   be   le - o   bi——— wa   be——— le

bi   wa   le   be   le - o   bi   wa   le   be——— le]

Chewing Gum Bubble

Purpose of the Exercise

To connect voice and body movement

A Brief History of the Exercise:

I learned this from Kevin Crawford in a voice workshop in my MA program at U.C.D. Drama Studies Centre in Dublin. I have modified it for young children and do it in theatre workshops for 8-11 year olds. They find it funny! — **Floortje Nyssen**

THE EXERCISE

1. Stand upright with your feet a little bit separated so that the legs go straight down from the hips and the knees are unlocked.

2. Imagine that you are in an enormous chewing gum bubble that increases and decreases in volume.

3. Try to move with the bubble while making a sound, but don't get stuck on the sticky wall of the chewing gum.

4. Now, while moving, begin vocalizing on a middle-pitch [a] as in "father."

5. Imagine the bubble growing bigger. Change your movement and sound to fit the new, bigger bubble.

6. Now, imagine the bubble growing smaller. Change your movement and sound to fit the new, smaller bubble.

7. As you change your movement and sound to fit the changing bubble, continue to breathe normally.

Note: *The breath awareness the students feel may surprise them.*

You may need to indicate when to change the sound in the beginning of the exercise, but soon the students will begin to change the sound spontaneously after a few seconds.

The sounds produced can be very surprising. You might want to make a recording of your students performing this exercise, then play it back to them.

Across the Floor

Purpose of the Exercise
To center the body, connect with breath, connect breath with sound, embody the sound, and strengthen support of the voice

A Brief History of the Exercise:
I adapted this from an exercise which, several years ago, Meredith Monk taught as part of her warm-up for a workshop in sound and movement. It has been modified and used successfully in undergraduate and graduate voice and text classes as a quick and lively warm-up which focuses the breath and engages the voice.
— **Karen Ryker**

THE EXERCISE   **CD: TRACK 19**

1. Stand with your back against a wall.

2. Select a destination on the opposite end of the room, directly across from where you are standing.

3. Move across the floor to your destination and think of moving your body and voice through space toward the destination.

4. Repeat Steps 1 and 2, then move across the floor to your destination in the following ways:

   a. On one breath, on an extended [s].

   b. On one breath, on a low-pitched [mmu], adding port-de-bras movement of the arms, to engage your body in the activity.

   c. Go up a step in pitch and, still swinging your arms, walk quickly to your destination.

   d. Turn around so that you are facing the wall. Go up another step in pitch and move backwards. Think of the sound moving your body backwards like a jet of air pushing you toward your destination.

Note: *If doing this with a group, you may want to ask some students to act as "spotters" to guide the students when they are walking backwards.*

   e. Turn back around so that your back is against the wall. Go up another step in pitch and stand on the tips of your toes, reaching up and forward, and move to your destination.

   f. Go up another step in pitch and leap every few steps to your destination.

Across the Floor

g. Go up another step in pitch and move to your destination as if electric shocks were hitting you.

h. Go up another step in pitch and wriggle across the room to your destination, making the sound wriggle, too.

i. Go up another step in pitch and pop across the room to your destination, making the sound pop, too.

j. With each step, take a new breath and stretch your body on a new vowel sound to your destination.

Emotional Flow

Purposes of the Exercise

To release the constriction of voice sometimes experienced in tension-held emotions

To help the actor meet the "emotional demands" (i.e. rage, glee or terror) inherent in some texts

A Brief History of the Exercise:

This exercise was inspired by the movement work of Jean Sabatine in her book Movement for Stage and Screen. *Sabatine delineates the physical application of emotional flow, finding energy states that elicit emotional identification through working outside-in (vibratory energy = nervousness or excitement) or inside-out (remembering an event in which one identifies the emotional state, allowing the emotional state to lead to a recognition of the physical usage and energy quality, a la Laban analysis). For example, happy childhood memories might lead to a swinging movement.* — **Lisa Wilson**

THE EXERCISE

Pre-Exercise Preparation

This exercise works best mid-way through the rehearsal process, as the exercise ends with the actors taking what they've learned into the "confines" of the stage setting. Have actors who are in a scene together work together for this exercise.

1. Pick a scene from the play that you would like to work on.

2. Now, on your own, identify the primary emotions of your character in that scene.

3. Come together in a circle.

4. Starting with you, name your character's primary emotions in the scene. Then, voice the emotion, using open vowel sounds and physicalizing the emotion. For example, sorrow might be expressed through a moaning, "moh" sound, and might be physicalized by rubbing the fist in the solar plexus or crawling on the floor.

5. Continue around the circle until each of you has named your character's primary emotions, then voiced the emotions using open vowel sounds, while physicalizing the emotions.

6. Now, get together with an actor with whom you share moments in the scene.

7. Begin interacting with one another using the emotional text only. The emotional text is the open vowel sound and physicalization you established for your character's primary emotion.

8. Now, begin the scene again, this time using the actual text. Act the scene using the same heightening of your character's emotions. Continue using open vowel sounds and physicalization throughout

Emotional Flow

the scene. Concentrate on emotions that are evoked by thwarted or won objectives, and those that are displayed for the purposes of winning.

9. Now, let's repeat the scene again, within the "confines" of the staging. Try to allow the open vowels and physicalization of the emotions to live in the scene.

Post-Exercise Discussion

What were each of you aware of vocally, physically and emotionally?

How did this change when you used the actual text of the scene?

How was this exercise useful to you?

Note: *The actor often finds their emotional flow during the other actor's actions as being strong or stronger than those in his/her own character's text. This is because the actions of the other actor influence our emotional flow.*

During post-exercise discussion, it is best to concentrate on what worked first, then to concentrate on what did not work. You can then challenge the actors to work on things that did not work the next time they perform this exercise.

Chapter 10

Exploring Character Voices and Dialects

Being able to make vocal adjustments is an important part of the actor's talent. Actors are frequently called upon to do off-camera character voices for television, radio, or film. They are also frequently asked to play characters who speak with regional dialects or foreign accents. All of this requires versatility and the ability to transform one's own vocal sound.

Patrick Fraley's "The Mendlshon Twins Exercise" (10-1) provides an opportunity for students to explore a wide variety of character voices while having fun. Christa Ray's transformative "Developing Harmonic Timbre Through the Animal Matrix" (10-2) is based on a Paul Newhams's "Voice Movement Therapy." In this astonishing work, we are encouraged to explore a variety of vocal timbres by actually changing the configuration of the vocal tract.

By working from the 'outside-in,' Erica Tobolski's "The Portrait Project" (10-3) uses postcards, paintings, and photographs to help the actor discover a character voice. And finally, Doug Honorof's fun-filled "Boxer-Briefs" (10-4) helps actors imitate speech, hone auditory memory, and speak a new accent or dialect.

The Mendlshon Twins Exercise

Purpose of the Exercise

To practice imitating character voices

A Brief History of the Exercise:

Creating character voices for animation and advertising has a lot to do with imitating others. I was looking for an exercise for my students that would give them some practice at imitating voice, while at the same time possessing the ever-important fun factor. This is a hoot. — **Patrick Fraley**

THE EXERCISE

This exercise takes about 15 minutes to complete. It is a partner exercise.

1. Have your partner prepare to perform three different, silly character voices.

2. The scene takes place at an identical twins convention. You and your partner, i.e. twin, are talking to an audience at the convention. While using his or her character voice, begin the scene by having your partner briefly introduce the two of you as identical twins.

3. Join in, portraying your partner's twin. Try to sound and act exactly like your "identical twin." In other words, mirror your partner's character voice.

4. You and your partner should spend a couple of minutes on each set of character voices.

5. You can switch with your partner after he or she has finished the three character voices or simply take turns initiating different character voices.

Developing Harmonic Timbre Through the Animal Matrix

Purposes of the Exercise

To project or extend sound

To expand vocal trac and increase control and flexibility of the vocal tract

To produce various vocal timbres

A Brief History of the Exercise:

This is a Voice Movement Therapy exercise. VMT was originally founded by Paul Newham. In Voice Movement Therapy, being able to expand the voice tube dimensions is the single most important part of the physical voicework. The expanded tube enables all the other vocal ingredients to be reverberated, amplified, and enhanced. Expanding the tube allows for the revealing of a vast color palette of emotions through the voice. Expanding the tube means expanding the self, making it central to the healing process This exercise provides a method for increasing control and flexibility of the vocal tract, giving one access to various vocal timbres, which can be employed in singing various song styles or for creating vocal characters. — ***Christa Ray***

THE EXERCISE

1. Stand erect with your legs straight, spine stretched vertically, arms hanging by your sides, and your eyes focused directly in front.

2. Imagine that your voice is a very narrow tube extending from the lips down to the indent between the clavicles and the top of the breastbone. This is the Flute Configuration (larynx high in the throat) of the vocal tract, which produces the Flute Timbre. Begin breathing in and out through the mouth, blowing cool air as though you were lowering the temperature of hot food. The mouth should be slightly pursed as in whistling. This position is called *Homo erectus* and represents the sophisticated, cognitive, and articulate human being.

3. As you breathe, maintain a facial expression of extreme concentration as you focus on your thoughts and the sensations inside your head. Now begin to vocalize in Flute Timbre, singing up and down your pitch range, exploring varying degrees of loudness in both modal and falsetto registers.

4. Now, relax the knees and drop your pelvis towards the ground, allowing the arms to float slightly out from the body. Curve the spine into a concave arc with the center of the chest imploded.

5. Continue to breathe in and out through the mouth but allow the voice tube to widen and lengthen down to the center of the torso at the bottom of the breastbone. Imagine that you are steaming up a window or a pair of sunglasses and feel how the expired breath is now warm. This is the Clarinet Configuration (larynx in the middle of the throat), which produces the Clarinet Timbre.

Developing Harmonic
Timbre Through the Animal Matrix

6. As you begin to vocalize through your pitch range in Clarinet Timbre, allow your facial expressions to relax (especially your jaw), your eyes to wander into peripheral vision. Shift the emphasis from a concentration of thought in the head to an awareness of the feelings residing in your heart. This position is called the Primate Position and provides an opportunity to identify with the great ape. You can explore singing and sounding with a relaxed, childlike curiosity and openness, giving voice to the sentiments of your heart space.

7. Now drop forward on the hands and knees, letting your abdomen relax and your belly hang down. Lower your center of experience into the belly to connect with your gut instincts. Allow the voice tube to expand to its maximum dimensions. Dilate the mouth and throat as though yawning and imagine that the tube extends from the lips all the way down into the belly. This is the Saxophone Configuration (larynx is low in the throat), which produces the Saxophone Timbre. This body position is called the Feline-Canine Position and provides an opportunity to identify with both the great cat (tiger, lion, leopard) and the wolf.

8. As you breathe, gulp the air in large quantities as though you were extremely thirsty and feel the air expanding the belly and abdominal cavity. Notice how taking in a large volume of air influences your feelings and sensations. As you contact the primal feelings in your instinctive center, give voice and melody to the energy in your guts. Explore your full pitch range in Saxophone Timbre, with varying degrees of loudness in modal and falsetto registers. As you sing you can flex your spine like a cat, arching your head and buttocks up and then dropping your head and pressing your upper back to the ceiling. Make sure the breath is dropping into the belly as you inhale and that your abdomen muscles are contracting and lifting your belly towards your spine on the exhalation.

9. Now, come up towards a standing position but bend over from the waist and raise your arms behind you as though they are wings. Continue to vocalize in Saxophone Timbre, but make the nasal sound by allowing some airflow to come up behind the soft palate into the nasal passages. This quality of nasality is called Violin in the Voice Movement Therapy system. Violin can be added into the Flute, Clarinet or Saxophone Timbres. This body position is called the Bird Position and provides an opportunity to identify with the great bird.

Violin brings to the voice a certain hardness and density, enabling the voice to be projected over greater distances and to be heard above other noise.

Developing Harmonic Timbre Through the Animal Matrix

Indigenous singing styles tend to have a lot of Violin in the voice because they developed in the open air where people had to sing to each other over large distances. Vocalizing with Violin is very supportive in developing strength in one's sound for projection on stage.

10. Now that you have identified the physicality and vocal quality of each animal position, travel through the cycle, moving from *Homo erectus* (Flute) to Primate (Clarinet), from Primate into Feline-Canine (Saxophone), from Feline-Canine into Bird (Violin), from Bird to Primate and from Primate back to *Homo erectus*. Vocalize the range of instinctive passions which arise as you pass through the Animal Matrix.

11. Now, as you continue to pass through the Animal Matrix, begin to personalize your exploration by following your empathy for other animals: reptiles, bovines, rodents as well as mythical creatures composed of various beastly qualities. Allow your voice and imagination to journey to places that tap into the primality and animality of your being.

12. Then, as your voice-movement safari approaches completion, return to the Animal Matrix of *Homo erectus*, Primate, Feline-Canine and Bird and settle where you started in the erect position of the articulate human being. Listen to the change of harmonic timbre as you move through the positions.

13. As you work with this exercise, your voice will grow so that your full pitch range can be expressed in each timbre through both your modal and falsetto registers.

The Portrait Project

Purpose of the Exercise

To create character voice

A Brief History of the Exercise:

I created this exercise to help the actor develop an inner life from an external source, using an image (portrait/photograph) to stimulate the imagination.

— ***Erica Tabolski***

THE EXERCISE

An "outside-in" approach, the goal is to utilize all the senses and stimuli available to the actor to create an original personality. The process allows the actor to move back and forth between intuitive and analytical modes of thinking in a playful, spontaneous way. Building on a series of steps, the actor connects from image to physicality to emotion to vocal expression to speech. The resultant "voice" expresses the essence of the personality and the words arise from the physical expression of a mind/body integration.

Pre-Exercise Preparation

Before you begin the exercise, place paintings and/or photographs on a table. I use postcards of paintings and photographs.

1. From the paintings/photographs on the table, choose an image that is compelling to you.

2. Find an aspect of this image and re-create it with your body. It may be a posture, an expression, or an energy.

3. Begin moving about in this body, exaggerating this characteristic. Try standing, sitting, walking, etc.

4. Begin to notice the room through these eyes. What are you drawn to? Do you see textures? Light vs. dark? Are you comfortable in this space? Do you want to hide?

5. Begin to notice others in the room, but do not interact with them yet.

6. Notice what other characteristics arise in you, both physically and emotionally.

7. Find a sound that expresses what you are experiencing internally. Let the sound evolve into a word or phrase.

The Portrait Project

8. Continue exploring the room and observing others while speaking this word or phrase.

9. Let the word or phrase extend into a running inner monologue, spoken out loud to yourself. Keep connecting to physical life, postures and movement as you speak out loud.

10. What is your viewpoint of the others? What is your status?

11. Begin interacting with others in the room, leading into conversations. If you find yourself slipping out of character or back into your own physical and vocal patterns, re-connect with the first image/posture and sound you created.

Note: *This exercise can be tailored for a specific voice exploration by asking the students to choose an image that is most unlike them, of a different gender, or their secret self.*

Extended improvisations, reflecting specific situations or tasks, can be suggested by the instructor.

Boxer-Briefs

Purpose of the Exercise

To help actors gain skill in imitating speech, honing auditory memory, and speaking in a new accent within a spontaneous communicative context before applying the accent to a text

A Brief History of the Exercise:

I created it from an inspiration when coaching a Pinter play at Yale.

— **Doug Honorof**

THE EXERCISE

Pre-Exercise Preparation

The accents are starting to sound fairly believable when you are imitating your primary source materials and exercising your springboard sentences, but I'd like to see us push the development of the voices for our characters a little further toward truthfulness by playing a game I call "Boxer-Briefs." In this game we are forced to make a transition between imitation, memory and communicating novel ideas of our own design while using the accent. This will help us connect more personally with the accent, and, I hope, will allow us to feel the accent in ourselves while communicating in a very truthful way. It will also force us to listen to the details of an accent especially carefully. Here's how it goes.

1. Let's all stand in a circle around the table. I'll start by turning to the person on my left and asking a very simple question in the target accent, "Do you wear boxers or briefs?"

2. Now s/he, for example, might answer, in accent, "Neither. I wear boxer briefs," if that were a truthful answer.

3. Then s/he would repeat the question, mimicking my tune, rhythm, voice quality, and body language, saying, "[The reader's name] asked me, 'Do you wear boxers or briefs?'"

4. Then s/he would add, "and I answered, 'Neither. I wear boxer-briefs.'"

5. Then s/he would turn to the person on his left and say, "Now what I want to know is..." and ask a question of his own.

6. Steps 2 through 5 we will iterate recursively as we go around the circle. In other words, before giving an answer, Actor C has to repeat Actor A's question to Actor B, Actor B's answer to Actor A, and Actor

Boxer-Briefs

B's new question. This is more than just a test of memory for words, though, because, as we repeat all these questions and answers, we imitate every detail of the original talker's speech and manner. By the time we get back around the circle, before answering the last question, Actor A will have to repeat his own original question and every other question and answer that have intervened. Obviously this first and last person is going to have a lot of these little bits to remember, but we'll all help out. Then, the first person to be asked a question (Actor B) gets to start the next round.

7. My question was a very silly question, but you are all more clever than I am and should be able to come up with some very entertaining open-ended questions that may lead us somewhere more interesting.

8. Great! Let's get started and listen carefully. If anyone misses a word or the tune goes awry or what-have-you, we can give each other notes.

Variation on the Exercise

Each questioner gets to choose his questionee.

Appendix

List of Contributors and Exercises

Argo, Betsy	Sign In
	I Can't Hear You
Armstrong, Eric	Defining the Vowel Space
Armstrong, Frankie	Gossip Hoeing
Barton, Robert	The Voice Speaks
Blaise, Cynthia	Throat and Neck Release on Sound
Brammer, Lynx	Neck Stretches
Brown, Oren	Inflection Exercise
Burke, Deena	Combining Nasal Resonance with the Creative Impulse
Burke, Kate	The Deal and The Truth
Corrigan, Mary	Breath Exercise
	Breath Journal
	Warm-Up Exercise for Breath & Body
Coy, Mary	Legs on the Chair Breathing Exercise
DeVore, Kate	Rest Position
Donohue, Tracy	Dueling Chorus
Dwyer, Mavourneen	Painting the Text
Fraley, Patrick	The Mendlshon Twins Exercise
Frye, Rinda	Healing Touch
Gang, Richard	The Medial [t]
Gist, Jan	Side Stretches at the Barre
Hale-Thomas, Deborah	Tongue on the Wet Part of the Lower Lip
Hampton, Marion	The Voice Outdoors
	Voice Leading the Body
Honorof, Doug	Boxer-Briefs
Houfek, Nancy	Advanced Triangle Pose with Partner
Johnson, Jim	Connections
Johnson, Marlene	Building a Wall
	The Glove Game
Kopf, Ginny	The "Hey!" Breath Exercise
Kur, Barry	The "Stupid" Exercise
Leeseberg-Lange, BettyAnn	Consonant Conga
Loree, Kristen	The Name Game
Lowry, Marya	Straw Work
	Giving Voice to Your Hunger
Mayer, Elizabeth	Gliding and Sliding

Appendix

List of Contributors and Exercises (continued)

Meier, Paul	To Glottalize or Not to Glottalize
Melton, Joan	The "Wailing" Routine
	Jog and Sound
Mennen, Dorothy Runk	Hum and Chew: Versions One and Two
	Honing the Toning
Merrit, Lorraine	Balance and Alignment Using the Wall
Metz, Elizabeth Carlin	The Conduit
Morris, Chrtistine	The Elephant Walking Chant
Moulton, Betty	Breathing Out the End of the Thought-Phrase
Nyssen, Floortje	Chewing Gum Bubble
Ray, Christa	Developing Harmonic Timbre Through the Animal Matrix
Rees, Mandy	Improvisation from Primitive Sound
	Key Word Ball Toss
Renaud, Lissa Tyler	Pitch Stretching
Richie, Chuck	Vocal Mirrors
Rodgers, Janet B.	The Anaconda
	Sirens
Rootberg, Ruth	Listening/Breathing Transition to Text
Ryker, Karen	Woo, Woe
	Quick Articulator Warm-Up
	Across the Floor
Scott, Jerrold	Singing Exercise for Line Melody
Stackhouse, Susan	Twelve-Step Program for Release of Neck, Jaws, and Shoulders
	The Speaker Exercise
Stewart, Natalie	Lessac's Consonant Orchestra Scenes
Thomas, Jennifer	The "Mommy" Exercise
Thompson, Annie	The "Ha"
Timberlake, Phil	Tennis Ball Torture
	The Wizard of Oz
Tobolski, Erica	The Portrait Project
Udall, Kate	Breath Flow
	Act Every Word
Van Den Berg, Elizabeth	Moving Sound
Watson, Lynn	Tell Me About the Time You...
Weiss, William	Awareness in the Sitting Position
Wilson, Lisa	Core Belief Exercise
	Emotional Flow

Appendix

CD Track Listing

Biographies

Betsy Argo is an adjunct faculty member at Roger Williams University in Rhode Island and a certified instructor in the Lessac Method of Voice and Diction.

Eric Armstrong teaches an eclectic approach to voice, dialects, and Shakespeare text at Roosevelt University in Chicago, and is director of Technology/Internet Services for the Voice and Speech Trainers Association (VASTA).

Frankie Armstrong has contributed chapters to six books, published an autobiography *As Far As the Eye Can Sing*, and recently co-edited *Well Tuned Women – Growing Strong Through Voicework*.

Robert Barton is head of the acting program at the University of Oregon. Robert is also the author of numerous scholarly articles and writes a regular column for *The Voice and Speech Review*. In 2002, he will teach for the American Heritage Program in London.

Cynthia Blaise is a voice, speech, and dialects coach, as well as an actor and director. Her film credits include *Spitfire Grill, Polish Wedding, Tecumseh,* and *The Affair of the Necklace.*

Lynx Brammer received her MFA in Theatre Education from Virginia Commonwealth University in 2000. She teaches workshops at Northern Stage in White River Junction, Vermont.

Oren Brown is Voice Faculty Emeritus at the Julliard School, where he has taught for nineteen years. He is the recipient of the Distinguished Service Award for contributions to the teaching profession and author of the book, *Discover Your Voice.*

Deena Burke is an Associate Professor at Cornish College of the Arts in Seattle, WA, where she heads the voice and speech component of the BFA Professional Actor Training Program. She is a graduate of the Julliard School and a VASTA board member.

Kate Burke is currently President of the Voice and Speech Trainers Association and head of the Voice program at the University of Virginia. Her acting credits include roles at the American Conservatory Theatre, the American Repertory Theatre, and other regional theatres.

Mary Corrigan is Emerita Professor at the University of California San Diego. She was one of twelve Rockefeller Grantees invited to study voice production with Kristin Linklater in 1965.

Mary Coy has taught at Shakespeare and Company in Lenox, MA, Syracuse University, University of Mississippi, Virginia Commonwealth University and is presently teaching at Randolph-Macon Women's College in Lynchburg, VA.

Kate DeVore teaches Voice for the Actor at Columbia College, works as a voice/speech pathologist at Gottfred Speech Associates, and runs a private practice in healing and voice enhancement and rehabilitation.

Tracy Donohue teaches Speech and Acting at East Carolina University. She received her MFA in Acting at the University of California, Davis. She also trained at the American Conservatory Theatre in San Francisco.

Mavoureen Dwyer teaches Voice/Speech and graduate level acting classes in Shakespeare and Period Acting Styles at the University of Arkansas, Fayetteville.

Patrick Fraley has created character voices for over 2500 cartoons, films, commercials, CD-ROMs, and Books on Audio projects. He is among the top ten performers of all time to be cast as a regular on animated TV shows.

A Practical Guide to
Child Care and Education Placements
2nd Edition

Christine Hobart
Jill Frankel

Series Editor: Miranda Walker

Nelson Thornes

First Edition published in 2002 by Nelson Thornes Ltd

This edition published in 2009 by:
Nelson Thornes Ltd
Delta Place
27 Bath Road
CHELTENHAM
GL53 7TH
United Kingdom

09 10 11 12 13 / 10 9 8 7 6 5 4 3 2 1

A catalogue record for this book is available from the British Library

ISBN 978 1 4085 0483 3

Illustrations by Jane Bottomley
Page make-up by Northern Phototypesetting Co. Ltd.
Printed and bound in Spain by GraphyCems